DATE DUE

MAY 16 2011		
NOV 05 2012		
MAR 3 0 2016 APR 1 3 2016		

Demco, Inc. 38-293

1st EDITION

Perspectives on Diseases and Disorders

Lupus

Hayley Mitchell Haugen
Book Editor

PERSPECTIVES
On Diseases & Disorders

GALE
CENGAGE Learning

Detroit • New York • San Francisco • New Haven, Conn • Waterville, Maine • London

Christine Nasso, *Publisher*
Elizabeth Des Chenes, *Managing Editor*

© 2010 Greenhaven Press, a part of Gale, Cengage Learning

Gale and Greenhaven Press are registered trademarks used herein under license.

For more information, contact:
Greenhaven Press
27500 Drake Rd.
Farmington Hills, MI 48331-3535
Or you can visit our Internet site at gale.cengage.com

For product information and technology assistance, contact us at

Gale Customer Support, 1-800-877-4253
For permission to use material from this text or product, submit all requests online at www.cengage.com/permissions

Further permissions questions can be e-mailed to permissionrequest@cengage.com

Articles in Greenhaven Press anthologies are often edited for length to meet page requirements. In addition, original titles of these works are changed to clearly present the main thesis and to explicitly indicate the author's opinion. Every effort is made to ensure that Greenhaven Press accurately reflects the original intent of the authors. Every effort has been made to trace the owners of copyrighted material.

Cover image copyright Custom Medical Stock Photo. Reproduced by permission.

LIBRARY OF CONGRESS CATALOGING-IN-PUBLICATION DATA

Lupus / Hayley Mitchell Haugen, book editor.
    p. cm. -- (Perspectives on diseases and disorders)
  Includes bibliographical references and index.
  ISBN 978-0-7377-4789-8 (hardcover)
  1. Lupus--Popular works. I. Haugen, Hayley Mitchell, 1968-
  RC312.5.S5L87 2010
  616.7'72--dc22
                                                         2009048653

Printed in the United States of America
1 2 3 4 5 6 7 14 13 12 11 10

CONTENTS

Rosalyn Carson-DeWitt

Systemic lupus erythematosus (SLE) is a disease of the immune system that causes that system to attack otherwise healthy organs and tissues. The causes of SLE remain mostly unknown, but various treatments for the disorder are available.

Rosalyn Carson-DeWitt

Discoid lupus erythematosus (DLE) is a disorder that causes red coin-shaped bumps to appear on the skin. Like systemic lupus, DLE is considered an autoimmune disorder that can be medically treated.

University of Maryland Medical Center

Researchers are unable to pinpoint a single cause of lupus, but they have discovered that viruses and exposure to chemicals and sunlight can trigger the disease. Genetics and the presence of autoantibodies in the immune system can also cause lupus.

CHAPTER 2 Perspectives into Lupus

CHAPTER 3 Personal Narratives

FOREWORD

"Medicine, to produce health, has to examine disease."
—Plutarch

Independent research on a health issue is often the first step to complement discussions with a physician. But locating accurate, well-organized, understandable medical information can be a challenge. A simple Internet search on terms such as "cancer" or "diabetes," for example, returns an intimidating number of results. Sifting through the results can be daunting, particularly when some of the information is inconsistent or even contradictory. The Greenhaven Press series Perspectives on Diseases and Disorders offers a solution to the often overwhelming nature of researching diseases and disorders.

From the clinical to the personal, titles in the Perspectives on Diseases and Disorders series provide students and other researchers with authoritative, accessible information in unique anthologies that include basic information about the disease or disorder, controversial aspects of diagnosis and treatment, and first-person accounts of those impacted by the disease. The result is a well-rounded combination of primary and secondary sources that, together, provide the reader with a better understanding of the disease or disorder.

Each volume in Perspectives on Diseases and Disorders explores a particular disease or disorder in detail. Material for each volume is carefully selected from a wide range of sources, including encyclopedias, journals, newspapers, non-fiction books, speeches, government documents, pamphlets, organization newsletters, and position papers. Articles in the first chapter provide an authoritative, up-to-date overview that covers symptoms, causes and effects, treatments, cures, and medical advances. The second chapter presents a substantial number of opposing viewpoints on controversial treatments and other current debates relating to the volume topic. The third chapter offers a variety of personal perspectives on the disease or disorder. Patients, doctors, caregivers, and loved ones represent just some of the voices found in this narrative chapter.

Each Perspectives on Diseases and Disorders volume also includes:

- An **annotated table of contents** that provides a brief summary of each article in the volume.
- An **introduction** specific to the volume topic.
- Full-color **charts and graphs** to illustrate key points, concepts, and theories.
- Full-color **photos** that show aspects of the disease or disorder and enhance textual material.
- **"Fast Facts"** that highlight pertinent additional statistics and surprising points.
- A **glossary** providing users with definitions of important terms.
- A **chronology** of important dates relating to the disease or disorder.
- An annotated list of **organizations to contact** for students and other readers seeking additional information.
- A **bibliography** of additional books and periodicals for further research.
- A detailed **subject index** that allows readers to quickly find the information they need.

Whether a student researching a disorder, a patient recently diagnosed with a disease, or an individual who simply wants to learn more about a particular disease or disorder, a reader who turns to Perspectives on Diseases and Disorders will find a wealth of information in each volume that offers not only basic information, but also vigorous debate from multiple perspectives.

INTRODUCTION

Systemic lupus erythematosus (SLE) is an autoimmune disorder that can affect many different parts of the body, including the skin, joints, heart, lungs, kidneys, and brain. In a normally functioning immune system, the body creates proteins called antibodies that fend off viruses, bacteria, and other foreign invaders known as antigens. People with lupus, however, have immune systems that do not differentiate between foreign substances like viruses and the body's healthy cells and tissues. When this happens, the antibodies created by the immune system (now referred to as autoantibodies) begin to work against the body itself. The main result of this process is painful inflammation that can damage multiple organs in the body and even cause life-threatening complications for people with lupus.

In 2009 the Lupus Foundation of America (LFA) estimated that approximately 1.5 million Americans have lupus. Anybody can get lupus, but the disorder primarily strikes women. In fact, nine out of ten people with lupus are women, generally within the childbearing ages of fifteen and forty-five. Women, thus, are of special interest to lupus researchers, and in the past sixteen years the focus of lupus research has also turned increasingly toward minority women. In the United States lupus is up to three times more common in African Americans and Hispanics than in Caucasians.

This statistic was discovered by physicians and public health experts Graciela S. Alarcón, Kemi Brooks, John D. Reveille, and Jeffrey R. Lisse in their 1999 paper "Do Patients of Hispanic and African-American Ethnicity with Lupus Experience Worse Outcomes than Patients

Nine out of ten lupus sufferers are women. The disease damages the body's organs and can become life-threatening.
(AP Images)

with Lupus from Other Populations?" Their research, which began in 1993 and was funded by the National Institutes of Health, became known as the LUMINA (LUpus in MInority populations: NAture vs. nurture) Study. LUMINA is the largest multiethnic, multiregional, and multi-institutional study of lupus to date. After following the cases of 229 patients with lupus, Reveille notes that he and his team of researchers discovered "mounting evidence that Hispanic and African American women have a higher incidence of lupus, more serious complications, and higher mortality rates" than Caucasian women with the disease.

Hispanic and African American patients with lupus tend to develop lupus earlier in life, experience greater disease activity, and have more medical complications attributed to the disorder than Caucasian patients. More specifically, according to the LUMINA study, African

American and Hispanic women are more likely to suffer renal (kidney) failure from lupus. Hispanic women in the group studied by LUMINA experienced a higher level of cardiac disease than other women. The African American women in the group acquired skin damage as a result of lupus more quickly than women of other ethnicities and also had a higher frequency of neurological problems such as seizures, hemorrhage, and stroke.

Because of the disparity of prognoses between Caucasian and minority women with lupus, John Williams, a staff writer for BlackDoctor.org, maintains that there remains an "urgent need for more education and research to address the fact that minority women are disproportionately impacted by the autoimmune disease lupus." Researchers tend to agree, as noted by their continuing focus on this issue. Williams, for example, refers to the 2004 expert panel discussion "Racial Disparities in Lupus: Strategies for Intervention in Minority Communities" at the 7th International Congress on SLE and Related Conditions. At this event Reveille emphasized that "three factors—disease activity, disease damage, and poverty—appear to be the most important determinants of mortality in multi-ethnic lupus patients in the US."

Elaborating on the issue of poverty, Williams reports that Ellen Ginzler, chief of rheumatology at SUNY Downstate Medical Center in New York, noted that the average annual cost to treat lupus is estimated at six thousand to ten thousand dollars per person. Depending on the severity of the disease, medications alone can cost several thousand dollars a month. Williams notes that hospitalizations and other treatments, such as dialysis for kidney failure, can add to these already exorbitant costs. The cost of treating lupus is just one factor to consider when thinking about lupus and minority women. Cultural differences, communication issues, levels of both familial and community support, and other factors also come into play.

While lupus in minority women remains a special concern to researchers and physicians, the viewpoints in the following chapters also introduce, discuss, and examine the disease, as well as the many other issues that surround it, in order to provide readers with a better understanding of lupus and its effects.

CHAPTER 1

Understanding Lupus

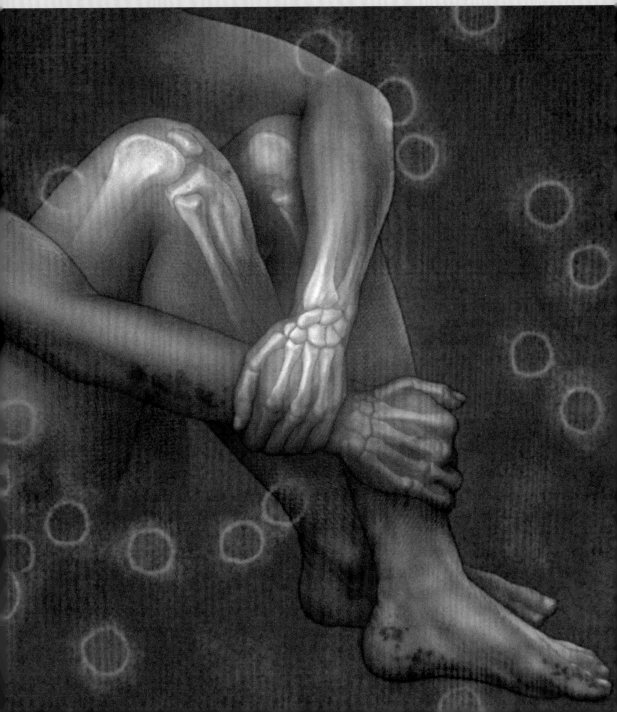

An Overview of Systemic Lupus Erythematosus

Rosalyn Carson-DeWitt

Rosalyn Carson-DeWitt writes and edits medical articles for print, Internet, and CD-ROM products. In the following article Carson-DeWitt provides an overview of systemic lupus erythematosus (SLE), a disease that causes the immune system to attack otherwise healthy organs and tissues. The causes of SLE remain mostly unknown, but its effects are well documented. Arthritis, skin rashes, and inflammation of the lungs are just a few of the medical problems that lupus can cause. Although lupus can be difficult to diagnose, various treatments for the disorder are available. The ultimate prognosis for lupus patients depends on the severity of their lupus activity, but early treatment can help most patients to live productive lives.

Photo on previous page. The two most common symptoms of systemic lupus erythematosus (SLE) are skin rashes and arthropathy, or joint disease. Both result from the abnormal immune system found in lupus patients. (John M. Daugherty/Photo Researchers, Inc.)

Systemic lupus erythematosus (also called lupus or SLE) is a disease where a person's immune system attacks and injures the body's own organs and tissues. Almost every system of the body can be affected by SLE.

SOURCE: Rosalyn Carson-DeWitt, *Gale Encyclopedia of Medicine,* Detroit: 2006. Copyright © 2006 Gale, a part of Cengage Learning Inc. Reproduced by permission of Gale, a part of Cengage Learning.

SLE and the Immune System

The body's immune system is a network of cells and tissues responsible for clearing the body of invading foreign organisms, like bacteria, viruses, and fungi. Antibodies are special immune cells that recognize these foreign invaders, and begin a chain of events to destroy them. In an autoimmune disorder like SLE, a person's antibodies begin to recognize the body's own tissues as foreign. Cells and chemicals of the immune system damage the tissues of the body. The reaction that occurs in tissue is called inflammation. Inflammation includes swelling, redness, increased blood flow, and tissue destruction.

In SLE, some of the common antibodies that normally fight diseases are thought to be out of control. These include antinuclear antibodies and anti-DNA antibodies. Antinuclear antibodies are directed against the cell's central structure that contains genetic material (the nucleus). Anti-DNA antibodies are directed against the cell's genetic material. DNA is the chemical substance that makes up the chromosomes and genes.

SLE can occur in both males and females of all ages, but 90% of patients are women. The majority of these women are in their childbearing years. African Americans are more likely than Caucasians to develop SLE.

Occasionally, medications can cause a syndrome of symptoms very similar to SLE. This is called drug-induced lupus. Medications that may cause this syndrome include hydralazine (used for high blood pressure) and procainamide (used for abnormal heartbeats). Drug-induced lupus almost always disappears after the patient stops taking the medications that caused it.

Causes and Symptoms

The cause of SLE is unknown. Because the vast majority of patients are women, some research is being done to determine what (if any) link the disease has to female hormones. SLE may have a genetic basis, although more

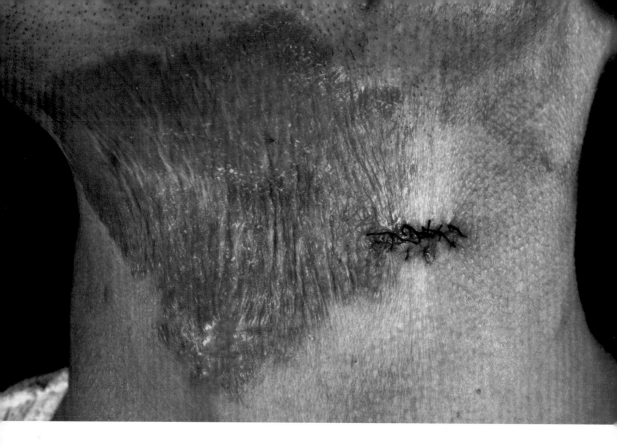

than one gene is believed to be involved in the development of the disease. Because patients with the disease may suddenly have worse symptoms (called a flare) after exposure to things like sunlight, alfalfa sprouts, and certain medications, researchers suspect that some environmental factors may also be at work.

The severity of a patient's SLE varies over time. Patients may have periods with mild or no symptoms, followed by a flare. During a flare, symptoms increase in severity and new organ systems may become affected.

Many SLE patients have fevers, fatigue, muscle pain, weakness, decreased appetite, and weight loss. The spleen and lymph nodes are often swollen and enlarged. The development of other symptoms in SLE varies, depending on the organs affected:

- Joints. Joint pain and problems, including arthritis, are very common. About 90% of all SLE patients have these types of problems.

- Skin. A number of skin rashes may occur, including a red butterfly-shaped rash that spreads across the face. The "wings" of the butterfly appear across the cheekbones, and the "body" appears across the bridge of the nose. A discoid, or coin-shaped, rash causes red, scaly bumps on the cheeks, nose, scalp, ears, chest, back, and the tops of the arms and legs. The roof of the mouth may develop sore, irritated pits (ulcers). Hair loss is common. SLE patients tend to be very easily sunburned (photosensitive).
- Lungs. Inflammation of the tissues that cover the lungs and line the chest cavity causes pleuritis, with fluid accumulating in the lungs. The patient frequently experiences coughing and shortness of breath.
- Heart and circulatory system. Inflammation of the tissue surrounding the heart causes pericarditis; inflammation of the heart itself causes myocarditis. These heart problems may result in abnormal beats (arrhythmias), difficulty pumping the blood strongly enough (heart failure), or even sudden death. Blood clots often form in the blood vessels and may lead to complications.
- Nervous system. Headaches, seizures, changes in personality, and confused thinking (psychosis) may occur.
- Kidneys. The kidneys may suffer significant destruction, with serious life-threatening effects. They may become unable to adequately filter the blood, leading to kidney failure.
- Gastrointestinal system. Patients may experience nausea, vomiting, diarrhea, and abdominal pain. The lining of the abdomen may become inflamed (peritonitis).
- Eyes. The eyes may become red, sore, and dry. Inflammation of one of the nerves responsible for vision may cause vision problems, and blindness can result from inflammation of the blood vessels (vasculitis) that serve the retina.

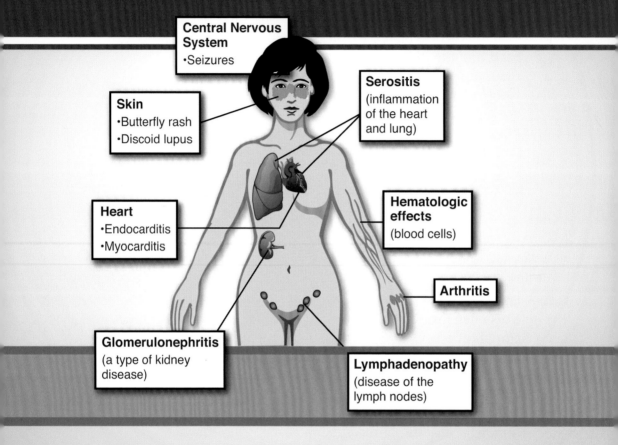

The Effects of Lupus

Nearly every system of the body can be affected by systemic lupus erythematosus (SLE).

Central Nervous System
•Seizures

Skin
•Butterfly rash
•Discoid lupus

Serositis
(inflammation of the heart and lung)

Heart
•Endocarditis
•Myocarditis

Hematologic effects
(blood cells)

Arthritis

Glomerulonephritis
(a type of kidney disease)

Lymphadenopathy
(disease of the lymph nodes)

Taken from: Rosalyn Carson-DeWitt, "Systemic Lupus Erythematosus," *Gale Encyclopedia of Medicine*, pp. 3616–3619, Gale Virtual Reference Library. Detroit: Gale, 2006.

Diagnosis

Diagnosis of SLE can be somewhat difficult. There are no definitive tests for diagnosing SLE. Many of the symptoms and laboratory test results of SLE patients are similar to those of patients with different diseases, including rheumatoid arthritis, multiple sclerosis, and various nervous system and blood disorders.

Laboratory tests that are helpful in diagnosing SLE include several tests for a variety of antibodies commonly elevated in SLE patients (including antinuclear antibodies, anti-DNA antibodies, etc.). SLE patients tend to have low numbers of red blood cells (anemia) and low numbers of certain types of white blood cells. The erythrocyte sedimentation rate (ESR), a measure of inflammation in the body, tends to be quite elevated. Samples of tissue (biopsies) from affected skin and kidneys show characteristics of the disease.

A test called the lupus erythematosus cell preparation (or LE prep) test is also performed. This test involves obtaining a sample of the patient's blood. Cells from the blood are damaged in the laboratory in order to harvest their nuclei. These damaged cells are then put together with the patient's blood serum, the liquid part of blood separated from the blood cells. Antinuclear antibodies within the patient's serum will clump together with the damaged nuclear material. A material called Wright's stain will cause these clumps to turn blue. These stained clumps are then reacted with some of the patient's white blood cells, which will essentially eat the clumps. LE cells are the white blood cells that contain the blue clumps. This test will be positive in about 70–80% of all patients with SLE.

The American Rheumatism Association developed a list of symptoms used to diagnose SLE. Research supports the idea that people who have at least four of the eleven criteria (not necessarily simultaneously) are extremely likely to have SLE. The criteria are:

- butterfly rash
- discoid rash
- photosensitivity
- mouth ulcers
- arthritis
- inflammation of the lining of the lungs or the lining around the heart

- kidney damage, as noted by the presence of protein or other abnormal substances called casts in the urine
- seizures or psychosis
- the presence of certain types of anemia and low counts of particular white blood cells
- the presence of certain immune cells, anti-DNA antibodies, or a falsely positive test for syphilis
- the presence of antinuclear antibodies

Treatment

Treatment depends on the organ systems affected by SLE and the severity of the disease. Some patients have a mild form of SLE. Their mild symptoms of inflammation can be treated with nonsteroidal anti-inflammatory drugs like ibuprofen (Motrin, Advil) and aspirin. Severe skin rashes and joint problems may respond to a group of medications usually used to treat malaria. More severely ill patients with potentially life-threatening complications (including kidney disease, pericarditis, or nervous system complications) will require treatment with more potent drugs, including steroid medications. Because steroids have serious side effects, they are reserved for more severe cases of SLE. Drugs that decrease the activity of the immune system (called immunosuppressant drugs) may also be used for severely ill SLE patients. These include azathioprine and cyclophosphamide.

Other treatments for SLE try to help specific symptoms. Clotting disorders will require blood thinners. Psychotic disorders will require specific medications. Kidney failure may require the blood to be cleaned outside the body through a machine (dialysis) or even a kidney transplantation.

Alternative Treatments

A number of alternative treatments have been suggested to help reduce the symptoms of SLE. These include acupuncture and massage for relieving the pain of sore joints and muscles. Stress management is key for people with SLE and such techniques as meditation, hynotherapy, and yoga may be helpful in promoting relaxation. Dietary suggestions include eating a whole foods diet with reduced amounts of red meat and dairy products in order to decrease pain and inflammation. Food allergies are believed either to contribute to SLE or to arise as a consequence of the digestive difficulties. Wheat, dairy products, and soy are the major offenders. An elimination/challenge diet can help identify the offending foods so that they can be avoided. Another dietary measure that may be beneficial is eating more fish that contain omega-3 fatty acids, like mackerel, sardines, and salmon. Because alfalfa sprouts have been associated with the onset of flares in SLE, they should be avoided. Supplements that have been suggested to improve the health of SLE patients include vitamins B, C, and E, as well as selenium, zinc, magnesium, and a complete trace mineral supplement. Vitamin A is believed to help improve discoid skin rashes. Botanical medicine can help the entire body through immune modulation and detoxification, as well as assisting individual organs and systems. Homeopathy and flower essences can work deeply on the emotional level to help people with this difficult disease.

> **FAST FACT**
>
> Lupus is more common than leukemia, muscular dystrophy, cerebral palsy, multiple sclerosis, and cystic fibrosis.

Prognosis

The prognosis for patients with SLE varies, depending on the organ systems most affected and the severity of inflammation. Some patients have long periods of time with mild or no symptoms. About 90–95% of patients are still living after 2 years with the disease. About 82–90% of patients are still living after 5 years with the disease. After 10 years, 71–80% of patients are still alive, and 63–75% are still alive after 20 years. The most likely causes of death during the first 10 years include infections and kidney failure. During years 11–20 of the disease, the most likely cause of death involves the development of abnormal blood clots.

Because SLE frequently affects women of childbearing age, pregnancy is an important issue. For pregnant SLE patients, about 30% of the pregnancies end in miscarriage. About 25% of all babies born to mothers with SLE are premature. Most babies born to mothers with SLE are normal. However, a rare condition called neonatal lupus causes a baby of a mother with SLE to develop a skin rash, liver or blood problems, and a serious heart condition.

Prevention

There are no known ways to avoid developing SLE. However, it is possible for a patient who has been diagnosed with SLE to prevent flares of the disease. Recommendations for improving general health to avoid flares include decreasing sun exposure, getting sufficient sleep, eating a healthy diet, decreasing stress, and exercising regularly. It is important for a patient to try to identify the early signs of a flare (like fever, increased fatigue, rash, headache). Some people believe that noticing and responding to these warning signs will allow a patient with SLE to prevent a flare, or at least to decrease its severity.

An Overview of Discoid Lupus

Rosalyn Carson-DeWitt

Rosalyn Carson-DeWitt writes and edits medical articles for print, Internet, and CD-ROM products. In this article Carson-DeWitt provides an overview of discoid lupus erythematosus (DLE), an autoimmune disorder that causes red coin-shaped bumps to appear on the skin. Like systemic lupus, there is no known cause for DLE, but it can be easily diagnosed by a skin biopsy. Patients with discoid lupus rarely develop systemic lupus, and the skin lesions associated with DLE are not life-threatening. Although discoid lupus cannot be prevented, it can be medically treated with a variety of creams and steroids, if necessary.

Discoid lupus erythematosus (DLE) is a disease in which coin-shaped (discoid) red bumps appear on the skin. The disease . . . only affects the skin, although similar discoid skin lesions can occur in the serious disease called systemic lupus erythematosus (SLE).

SOURCE: Rosalyn Carson-DeWitt, *Gale Encyclopedia of Medicine.* Detroit: Gale, 2006. Copyright © 2006 Gale, a part of Cengage Learning Inc. Reproduced by permission of Gale, a part of Cengage Learning.

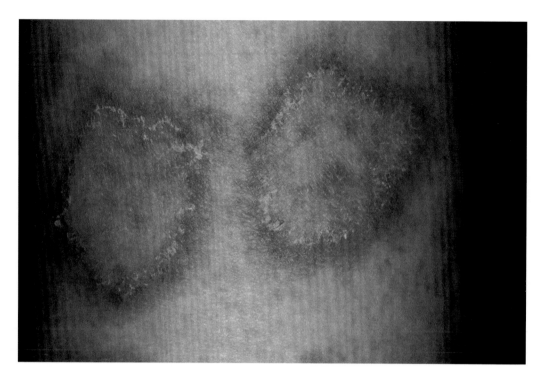

Skin lesions of discoid lupus are coin-shaped bumps appearing on the skin. The cause is not yet known. (Scott Camazine/Photo Researchers, Inc.)

Only about 10% of all patients with DLE will go on to develop the multi-organ disease SLE.

The tendency to develop DLE seems to run in families. Although men or women of any age can develop DLE, it occurs in women three times more frequently than in men. The typical DLE patient is a woman in her 30s.

Causes and Symptoms

The cause of DLE is unknown. It is thought that DLE (like SLE) may be an autoimmune disorder. Autoimmune disorders are those that occur when cells of the immune system are misdirected against the body. Normally, immune cells work to recognize and help destroy foreign invaders like bacteria, viruses, and fungi. In autoimmune disorders, these cells mistakenly recognize various tissues of the body as foreign invaders, and attack and destroy these tissues. In SLE, the misdirected immune cells are antibodies. In DLE, the damaging cells are believed to be a type of white blood cell called a T lymphocyte. The injury to the skin results in inflammation and the characteristic discoid lesions.

In DLE, the characteristic skin lesion is circular and raised. The reddish rash is about 5–10 mm in diameter, with the center often somewhat scaly and lighter in color

Discoid Lupus Rash

Lupus rash is red or purplish and mildly scaly, appearing on the face (butterfly or malar rash) and symmetrically on the arms, fingers, or legs.

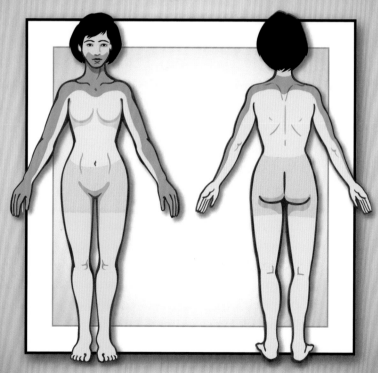

◯ **Most common**　⬤ **Common**　◯ **Uncommon**　◯ **Rare**

than the darker outer ring. The surface of these lesions is sometimes described as "warty." There is rarely any itching or pain associated with discoid lesions. They tend to appear on the face, ears, neck, scalp, chest, back, and arms. As DLE lesions heal, they leave thickened, scarred areas of skin. When the scalp is severely affected, there may be associated hair loss (alopecia).

People with DLE tend to be quite sensitive to the sun. They are more likely to get a sunburn, and the sun is likely to worsen their discoid lesions.

Diagnosis

Diagnosis of DLE usually requires a skin biopsy. A small sample of a discoid lesion is removed, specially prepared, and examined under a microscope. Usually, the lesion has certain microscopic characteristics that allow it to be identified as a DLE lesion. Blood tests will not reveal the type of antibodies present in SLE, and physical examination usually does not reveal anything other than the skin lesions. If antibodies exist in the blood, or if other symptoms or physical signs are found, it is possible that the discoid lesions are a sign of SLE rather than DLE.

Treatment of DLE primarily involves the use of a variety of skin creams. Sunscreens are used for protection. Steroid creams can be applied to decrease inflammation. Occasionally, small amounts of a steroid preparation will be injected with a needle into a specific lesion. Because of their long list of side effects, steroid preparations taken by mouth are avoided. Sometimes, short-term treatment with oral steroids will be used for particularly severe DLE outbreaks. Medications used to treat the infectious disease malaria are often used to treat DLE.

FAST FACT

Discoid lupus erythematosus may occur at any age but most often occurs in persons aged twenty to forty years.

Alternative Treatments

Alternative treatments for DLE include eating a healthy diet, low in red meat and dairy products and high in fish containing omega-3 fatty acids. These types of fish include mackerel, sardines, and salmon. Following a healthy diet is thought to decrease inflammation. Dietary supplements believed to be helpful include vitamins B, C, E, and selenium. Vitamin A is also recommended to improve DLE lesions. Constitutional homeopathic treatment [when one homeopathic medicine is used to treat a variety of symptoms] can help heal DLE as well as help prevent it [from] developing into SLE.

Prognosis

For the most part, the prognosis for people with DLE is excellent. While the lesions may be cosmetically unsightly, they are not life threatening and usually do not cause a patient to change his or her lifestyle. Only about 10% of patients with DLE will go on to develop SLE.

Prevention

DLE cannot be prevented. Recommendations to prevent flares of DLE in patients with the disease include avoiding exposure to sun and consistently using sunscreen.

The Causes of Lupus

University of Maryland Medical Center

The University of Maryland Medical Center publishes an online comprehensive and interactive medical reference library, including more than fifty thousand pages of medically reviewed health content. In this viewpoint the editors provide an in-depth examination of the possible causes of lupus. No one factor has been pinpointed as the single cause of lupus, but people with overactive immune systems are especially prone to the disorder. Genetic and hormonal factors may also play a role in the disease. Exposure to sunlight and other forms of ultraviolet light, as well as exposure to certain chemicals or the use of particular prescription drugs, can also trigger the immune system response that causes lupus.

Systemic lupus erythematosus (SLE) is a complex disorder that occurs as a consequence of a number of independent processes and factors.

Environmental factors, such as viruses, exposure to chemicals, or sunlight trigger inflammatory or immune ac-

SOURCE: University of Maryland Medical Center, "Systemic Lupus Erythematosus—Causes," www.umm.edu, January 21, 2008. Copyright © 2008 A.D.A.M. Inc. Reproduced by permission.

tivity. This immune activation may begin as an appropriate response to an unwanted "invader." But, because of a combination of genetic factors, an individual with lupus develops an ongoing immune response that does not shut itself off appropriately. This leads to waxing and waning flares of inflammation that can involve various organs of the body, depending on specific features of this self-perpetuating immune response in individual patients.

The exact combination of genes that predispose individuals to SLE may differ somewhat from patient to patient, but probably share certain common features which tend to impair the ability of the body to get rid of immune-triggering particles and which tend to prolong or increase the degree of immune responsiveness to these triggers.

A major characteristic of lupus is that it is an autoimmune response in which immune factors, called autoantibodies, attack the person's own cells. Some autoantibodies are normal in a well-balanced immune system, and serve various roles to help the body dispose of wastes,

A light micrograph of a human blood smear displays a systemic lupus erythematosus (SLE) infection. The nuclei of SLE-infected cells are stained in dark pink. (**SPL/Photo Researchers, Inc.**)

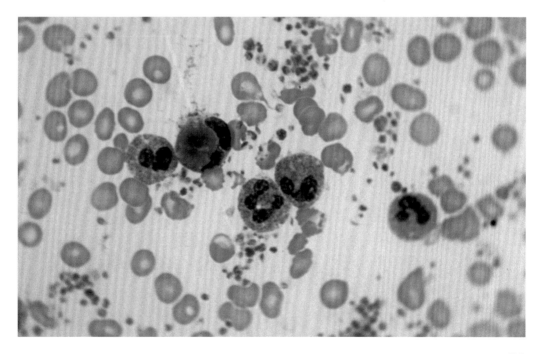

protect from infectious invaders, and to keep blood vessels clear. In healthy people, autoantibodies tend to be well-regulated and well "masked," or covered up, until needed. Therefore, it is probably the high activity and high detectability of autoantibodies that makes lupus unique, not the fact that they exist.

The Inflammatory Process and Autoimmunity

The Normal Immune System Response

The inflammatory process is a byproduct of the activity of the body's immune system, which fights infection and heals wounds and injuries:

- When an injury or an infection occurs, white blood cells are mobilized to rid the body of any foreign proteins, such as a virus.
- The masses of blood cells that gather at the injured or infected site produce factors to fight any infections.
- In the process, the surrounding area becomes inflamed and some healthy tissue is injured. The immune system is then called upon to repair wounds by clotting any bleeding blood vessels and initiating fiber-like patches to the tissue.
- Under normal conditions, the immune system has special factors that control and limit this inflammatory process.

The Infection Fighters

B cells and T cells are two important components of the immune system that play a role in the inflammation associated with lupus. Both B cells and T cells belong to a family of immune cells called lymphocytes. Lymphocytes help fight infection.

B cells and T cells are involved in the immune system's response to infection. Antigens are foreign bodies (such as bacteria and viruses) that stimulate the immune

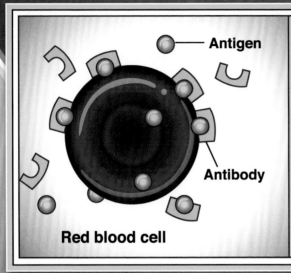

Antigen

An antigen is a substance that induces the formation of antibodies because it is recognized by the immune system as foreign to the body.

Antibody

Red blood cell

Taken from: University of Maryland Medical Center, "Systemic Lupus Erythematosus: Causes," January 21, 2008.

system to produce autoantibodies. When a T cell recognizes an antigen it will produce chemicals (cytokines) that cause B cells to multiply and release many immune proteins (antibodies). These antibodies circulate widely in the bloodstream, recognizing the foreign particles and triggering inflammation in order to rid the body of the invasion.

For reasons that are still not completely understood, both the T cells and B cells become overactive in lupus patients. In lupus, a complex interaction between activated immune cells and an impaired antigen-elimination process leads to a greater than normal range of what the antibodies recognize. Eventually, antibodies are made that recognize more of the body's own tissues in a stronger or more persistent manner than is healthy, and inflammatory responses are mounted in these tissues.

Autoantibodies

In the majority of patients with SLE, antinuclear antibodies (ANA) are detectable. Such autoantibodies may be present in individuals up to 7 years prior to their developing symptoms of lupus. Some subtypes of ANA are found in lupus patients and only rarely in people without lupus. These include:

- Anti-ds DNA. An autoantibody called anti-double-stranded DNA (anti-ds DNA) may play an important role in some lupus patients.
- Anti-Sm antibodies. This antibody is found most often in lupus patients of African descent and is almost never detected in people without lupus.
- Anti-Ro (SSA) and Anti-La (SSB)
- Antiphospholipid antibodies

Cytokines

Most immune cells secrete or stimulate the production of powerful immune factors called cytokines. In small amounts, cytokines are indispensable for maintaining the balance of the body during immune responses, including:

- Infections
- Injuries
- Tissue repair
- Blood clotting
- Clearing of debris from inflamed blood vessels
- Other aspects of healing

If overproduced, however, they can cause serious damage, including dangerous levels of inflammation and cellular injury. Specific cytokines called interferons and interleukins play a critical role in SLE by regulating the secretion of autoantibodies by B cells.

Complement

Another immune factor of high interest in SLE is the complement system. This is comprised of more than 30 proteins and is important for defending and regulating the immune response. . . .

Genetic Defects

Researchers estimated that 20–100 different genetic factors may be involved in the alterations of the immune system set point that could make a person susceptible to SLE.

- Research published in 2003 identified a particular set of genes, now commonly called the "interferon signature," that is activated by interferon in patients with severe lupus. This discovery may help doctors identify patients at particular risk for severe disease before they develop symptoms.
- A genetic risk factor for lupus in African-American women has been identified.
- Other research has identified defects in genes that regulate apoptosis, the natural process by which cells self-destruct.
- An abnormal gene identified in some patients with SLE promotes the build-up of immune complexes that can cause kidney damage. . . .

Triggers of the Immune Response

In genetically susceptible people, there are various external factors that can provoke an immune response. Possible SLE triggers include colds, fatigue, stress, chemicals, sunlight, and certain drugs.

Viruses
Blood tests reveal that patients with SLE are more likely to have been exposed to certain viruses than the general population. These viruses include the Epstein-Barr virus (the cause of mononucleosis), cytomegalovirus, and parvovirus-B1.

Results from a 2005 study, conducted by researchers at the National Institute of Environmental Health Sciences, suggested a strong association between Epstein-Barr virus (EBV) and increased risk of lupus, particularly for African-Americans. The association was not as strong for whites, but increased with age (patients over 50 years of age had four times higher risk). . . .

Some research suggests that different viruses may imprint specific types of SLE. For instance cytomegalovirus may affect blood vessels and cause problems such as Raynaud's phenomenon or blood abnormalities, but may not affect the kidney as much. These are speculations, however, and not a proven association.

Sunlight

Ultraviolet (UV) rays found in sunlight are important SLE triggers. When they bombard the skin, they can alter the structure of DNA in cells below the surface. The immune system may perceive these altered skin cells as foreign and trigger an autoimmune response against them. UV light is categorized as UVB or UVA depending on the length of the wave.

- UVB are short waves (280–320 nm [nanometer]). The shorter the wavelengths, the more damage they do.
- UVA are longer waves (320–400 nm). Some research suggests that UVA wavelengths in the longest range, know as UVA1 (340–400 nm), may actually repair DNA and normalize immune responses.

Chemicals

Clusters of SLE cases have occurred in populations with high exposure to certain chemicals. Chlorinated pesticides and crystalline silica are two suspects. A number of other chemicals are under investigation. However, it is very difficult to determine a causal role for any specific chemicals. (Silicone breast implants have been under intense scrutiny as a possible trigger of autoimmune diseases, including SLE. The weight of evidence to date, however, finds no support for this concern.) Some drugs have been associated with a temporary lupus syndrome (drug-induced lupus), which resolves when these drugs are stopped.

Hormones

Cytokines, major immune factors that are active in SLE, are directly affected by sex hormones. In general, estrogen enhances antibody production, and testosterone reduces antibody production, although their exact role in SLE may be more complicated than that since there are various ways in which each hormone might influence various immune cells. Women with SLE may have lower levels of several active male hormones (androgens), and some men who are affected by SLE may also have abnormal androgen levels.

> **FAST FACT**
>
> Temporary, drug-induced lupus may be caused by the following prescription drugs: hydralazine (used to treat high blood pressure), procainamide (used to treat irregular heart rhythms), and isoniazid (used to treat tuberculosis).

Premature menopause, and its accompanying symptoms (such as hot flashes), is common in women with SLE. Hormone replacement therapy (HRT), which is used to relieve these symptoms, increases the risk for blood clots and heart problems. It is not clear whether HRT triggers SLE flares. Women should discuss with their doctors whether HRT is an appropriate and safe choice. Guidelines recommend that women who take HRT use the lowest possible dose for the shortest possible time. Women with SLE who have active disease, antiphospholipid antibodies, or a history of blood clots or heart disease should not use HRT.

Oral Contraceptives

Female patients with lupus used to be cautioned against taking oral contraceptives (OCs) due to the possibility that estrogen could trigger lupus flare-ups. However, recent evidence indicates that OCs are safe, at least for women with inactive or stable lupus. Women who have been newly diagnosed with lupus should avoid OCs. Lupus can cause complications in its early stages. For this reason, women should wait until the disease reaches a stable state before taking OCs. In addition, women who have a history of, or who are at high risk for, blood clots should not use OCs. The estrogen in OCs increases the risk for blood clots.

The Symptoms of Lupus

Michelle Meadows

Michelle Meadows is a staff writer for *FDA Consumer* magazine, an online publication for healthy living from the Food and Drug Administration. Meadows examines the various ways in which day-to-day life for lupus patients can be a struggle. Three different patients illuminate just a few of the typical symptoms of lupus, including extreme fatigue, skin rashes, arthritic joint pain, and kidney problems. Meadows also reports on the stress, frustration, and depression these patients often encounter as they attempt to understand and come to terms with their disease.

Arletha Manlove, 41, of Kansas City, Mo., first noticed feeling different after having her first child. She experienced unusual fatigue, but thought maybe it was the adjustment of taking care of a new baby.

Everything was a struggle, she says. "It was a chore to take a shower and a chore to get dressed." She also had unexplained fevers, recurrent upper respiratory infections,

SOURCE: Michelle Meadows, "Battling Lupus," *FDA Consumer,* vol. 39, July/August 2005.

Arthritis

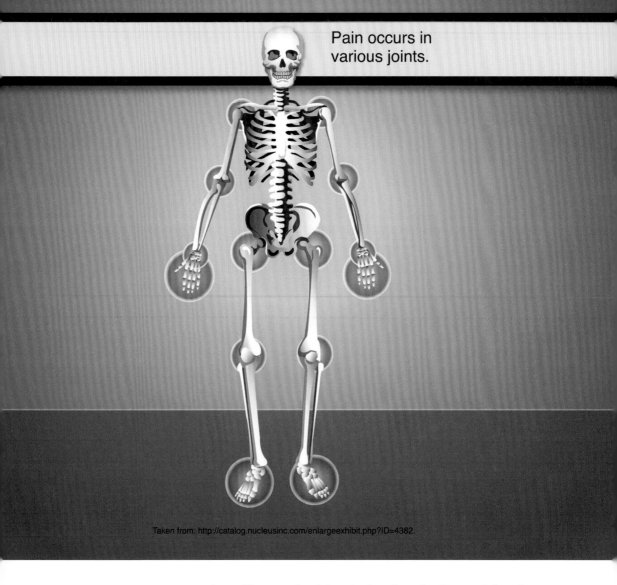

Pain occurs in various joints.

Taken from: http://catalog.nucleusinc.com/enlargeexhibit.php?ID=4382.

and swelling and aching in her hands. "I would wake up in the morning with swollen fingers, and by the time I got dressed, the swelling would go down."

She had six miscarriages in five years and repeated bouts of uterine pain. "I had been to gynecologists, psychiatrists, psychologists, and general practitioners," she says. "I started to think maybe they were right; maybe it was all in my head."

After a devastating miscarriage in the second trimester of pregnancy, Manlove's uterine pain became even worse and her other symptoms continued. At her mother's urging, she agreed to try one more doctor, a fertility specialist. He diagnosed her with both endometriosis and lupus in 1990 and referred her to a rheumatologist, a doctor who has additional training in diagnosing and treating arthritis and other diseases of the joints, muscles, and bones.

Manlove recalls feeling better right away after taking a combination of three medicines: prednisone, Imuran (azathioprine), and Plaquenil (hydroxychloroquine). "I remember thinking: 'I'm back! This is what it's like to feel good,'" she says. "But then the side effects kicked in. I had horrible mood swings, and within a very short time, I went from 121 pounds to 200 pounds."

Under close monitoring from her doctor, Manlove went on to have a successful pregnancy and had a second child 12 years ago. She says she's learned that good communication between patients and doctors is essential for coping with chronic illness. "I was very good about letting him know about side effects and asking questions, and we have been able to cut back on some of the medications over time," she says. She's also made important lifestyle changes. "You can't expect your doctor to give you a pill and then everything will be OK," she adds.

Patients Must Be Proactive to Fight Lupus

Lupus experts recommend that people with lupus have regular medical appointments and take their medication as prescribed. Other recommendations include sunscreen use and limiting sun exposure to prevent flares, regular exercise to improve joint flexibility and muscle strength, good eating habits, and plenty of rest.

"I've learned to stop when I need to, and sometimes I take three short naps in a day," says Manlove, who works full time and is active with the Lupus Foundation of America (LFA) as a support group facilitator. A chronic illness can take a toll on family and friends, too, so it's important to seek out support. "My husband believes me when I say I feel bad," she says. "Without his support, the stress of this journey would have been much harder. Not everyone is so lucky."

The body's natural defenses, called the immune system, protect us from viruses, bacteria, and other foreign invaders. But in people with systemic lupus erythematosus (SLE), the immune system can't tell the difference between foreign substances and the healthy cells and tissues. "Instead of fighting infection, the immune system attacks 'self,' the person's normal tissues," says Michelle Petri, M.D., a professor of medicine and director of the Lupus Center at The Johns Hopkins University School of Medicine in Baltimore. Immune complexes then build up in the tissues, causing inflammation, tissue injury, and pain. "SLE can affect any organ system," Petri says, "but especially causes skin rashes after sun exposure, swollen joints, and kidney disease."

SLE, also commonly called lupus, is a chronic autoimmune disease that affects 1.5 million to 2 million Americans, according to the LFA. Nine out of 10 people who have it are women, and it mostly affects women of childbearing age, those between ages 15 and 44. But men, children younger than 15, and older people also get lupus. People of any race or ethnicity can develop lupus, but blacks, Hispanics, Asians, and American Indians are at increased risk.

There is no cure for lupus, but, in most cases, the disease can be managed. Because of better detection and early treatment, between 80 percent and 90 percent of people with lupus can look forward to a normal lifespan, according to the LFA.

"Although the overall outlook has improved, it is a disease that must be monitored very carefully," says David Isenberg, M.D., academic director of rheumatology at University College London. "It has a major effect on quality of lives, and a smaller, but significant, number of people still die from it."

Maribel Ramirez, 43, was diagnosed with lupus in 1989 and started a support group in the Houston area in 1995 for Spanish speakers who have the disease. "I see people dying, and it's very difficult," she says. "We are desperate for better treatments." Ramirez has suffered damage to her lungs, kidneys, and heart. In 1994, she had a stroke due to vasculitis, a condition in which blood vessels become inflamed. "I worry about the disease and all the medications that I've been taking for so long," she says.

FAST FACT

Women die from lupus at five times the rate of men.

There are effective drugs that decrease inflammation and suppress the immune system in people with lupus, but these drugs also can lead to damaging side effects. Doctors and patients have to weigh carefully the benefits and risks of treatment. Isenberg likens treating patients with lupus to putting them on a fence between two fields. "One side represents the effects of the disease, and the other represents the side effects of treatment," he says. For example, people with lupus are at increased risk for developing hardening of the arteries that can cause a heart attack or stroke. The risk is due partly to having lupus and partly to taking corticosteroids, which decrease inflammation caused by the disease.

Another challenge, says Petri, is that there are no treatments for two common complaints of lupus patients—fatigue and memory loss. Ramirez says she once had to pull off the freeway and call a friend for help because she was lost, even though she was very close to home.

Lupus Symptoms Are Wide-Ranging

Researchers are looking for lupus treatments that are safer and more targeted, but the uniqueness of the disease poses challenges for drug development. The exact cause of lupus is unknown. The disease varies in intensity. And the symptoms are wide-ranging, sometimes involving multiple organs. Symptoms also tend to come and go, with active periods, called flares, and quiet periods when the disease is in remission.

In March 2005, the Food and Drug Administration released a draft guidance for industry on testing drugs for lupus in clinical trials. The guidance includes a general discussion of outcomes and measurements of disease activity, as well as claims that the agency may be willing to approve if they are supported by substantial evidence. "This guidance is an important step in stimulating new drug development for lupus treatment," says Acting FDA Commissioner Dr. Lester M. Crawford. "We are intensely interested in this area."

The most common symptoms of lupus are skin rashes, extreme fatigue, arthritis, unexplained fevers, and kidney problems. According to the LFA, about 40 percent of people with lupus have a rash that spreads across the nose and over the cheeks in the shape of a butterfly, called the malar rash.

"Because lupus can affect any organ, the disease can look different in different people," says David Wofsy, M.D., chief of rheumatology at the San Francisco Veterans Affairs Medical Center and professor of medicine at the University of California, San Francisco. Inflammation in one person might lead to multiple organ damage, whereas another person might have just occasional joint pain. "There are many people who never encounter the life-threatening manifestations of the disease," Wofsy says.

When lupus is severe, such as with serious kidney damage, the symptoms are more obvious to a physician. But, in most cases, people experience mild symptoms, which can make the illness hard to diagnose. Lupus also may develop gradually. "In the hands of someone knowledgeable about lupus, it can be easy to diagnose," Wofsy says. "But it's not uncommon to hear that someone with lupus went to several doctors before being diagnosed or was misdiagnosed." Experts say that sometimes, it can take a couple of years to figure out what's going on.

"In mild forms of the disease, symptoms usually present in a confusing manner," Wofsy says. "Somebody comes in who is young with a variety of nonspecific symptoms, and a doctor may not be thinking about lupus. The person might complain about feeling tired in the afternoons or about feeling achy. A doctor could think that these symptoms might be due to stress or depression, or a virus."

One of the most frustrating things for someone with lupus is being sick, but feeling like nobody believes you,

Shown here is a specimen of human kidneys infected with systemic lupus erythematosus. (**CNRI/Photo Researchers, Inc.**)

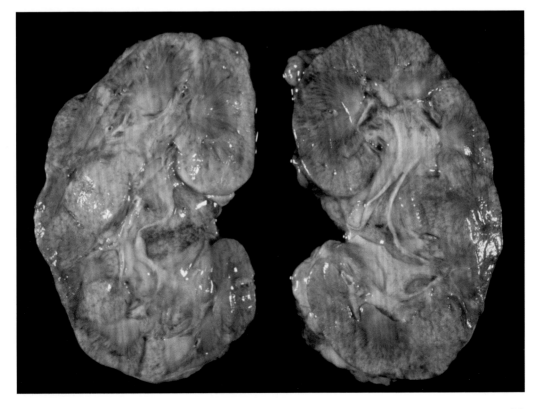

Ramirez says. "People think you're lazy or crazy, or both," she says. "You can also look nice and healthy, even though you feel very bad."

Before she was diagnosed with lupus, Ramirez battled mysterious symptoms for 10 years. She had five miscarriages, and later found out that women with lupus have higher rates of pregnancy loss. She also had unexplained skin rashes, anemia, pain in her legs and arms, urinary tract infections, kidney infections, fevers, mouth sores, and overwhelming fatigue.

Fatigue Is Worrisome for Lupus Patients

In an unpublished study done in 1999, Isenberg and his colleagues asked 100 lupus patients what they were most worried about regarding their illness. "Their biggest concern was fatigue," Isenberg says. "They were worried about sleeping all night and still being exhausted in the morning or about feeling too tired to pick their children up from school or to do other things that they want to do."

As a former police officer and member of the military, Tony Chisholm, 46, of Fall City, Wash., was used to being active. Feeling wiped out from lupus sent him into a deep depression. "I just couldn't get out of bed," he says. "But nothing would show up on a physical exam." He also has had bouts of flu symptoms, swelling around the eyes, joint pain, and chest pain. "Sometimes, the symptoms last for four months, and then I might go four more months without any problems," he says.

It was a photograph that finally helped Chisholm get some answers. In 1997, he and his family went to Great Britain for vacation and met another couple. The couple mailed Chisholm a photo from the trip. "The red butterfly rash across my face was plain as day," he says. "My wife insisted that I go to the doctor." After looking at the photo, the doctor ran tests for lupus. "Before that, I hadn't been diagnosed with anything else, except maybe hypochondria."

Lupus Patients Must Be Vigilant About Infections

Donald E. Thomas Jr.

Donald E. Thomas Jr. is a rheumatologist who serves as an active member of the Medical and Scientific Advisory Board of the Lupus Foundation of America. In this viewpoint Thomas encourages lupus patients to learn as much as they can about their disease and to play an active role in their own health care. He especially warns lupus sufferers to be vigilant about infections, as infections can cause many complications for lupus patients and even contribute to the deaths of 20 to 50 percent of lupus sufferers. Because of this risk, lupus patients need to take care to prevent infections when possible, and they need to seek immediate medical care should an infection occur.

I'm a strong believer that patients with lupus who learn as much as they can about their condition and play an active role in their health care do best in the long run. Treatments for systemic lupus erythematosus (SLE) have improved substantially over the past few decades. Before antibiotics and steroids became available,

SOURCE: Donald E. Thomas Jr., "Infections and Lupus," *Lupus Mid-Atlantic*, www.lupusmd.org. Reproduced by permission.

the vast majority of patients with SLE died within the first 2 years of the disease. Now, 80% of patients can expect to live well past 10 years. In fact, the majority of those with mild disease, with no major internal organ involvement, can plan on living normal life spans as long as they keep up with their health care to help their lupus and its potential complications remain under control. Knowing what those potential complications can be is the first step in knowing what to do. Infections are a major potential complication in patients with SLE.

When we look at patients who die from SLE or its complications, these deaths occur in two time periods marked by different causes of death. The first period is the first couple of years after their diagnosis. The vast majority of patients who die during this period do so from a combination of the lupus itself and major infections. These infections are due to the abnormal immune systems these patients have due to their lupus coupled with the suppression of their immune systems from the medications that are needed in order to treat their lupus. These are generally patients who have severe lupus, usually with involvement of major organs such as kidney, lung, heart, or brain. The second period occurs after the first couple of years; cardiovascular disease with strokes, heart attacks, and blood clots become the major cause of death, followed closely by infections.

As one can see, infections are an important potential cause of death at any time during the life of a lupus patient. It is estimated that somewhere between 20% and 50% of all lupus patients will have an infection as a contributing role in their death. This is why it is so important to know how to prevent, identify, and treat infections in patients who have SLE.

So just what is an infection? An infection is when another organism, commonly called a "germ," gets into the body, uses the body for nourishment, multiplies, and causes damage to the body. The immune system, most

importantly white blood cells, sees these invaders and attacks them in order to protect the body. This battle between the germs and the immune system ends up causing inflammation. The hallmarks of inflammation are redness, heat, swelling, and pain. Just think of what happens after exposure to poison ivy. The areas of uncomfortable, warm, red swellings are the result of inflammation from the immune system reacting to the poison of the poison ivy plant. A similar thing happens with infection. For example, strep throat (due to infection from streptococcus bacteria in the back of the throat) causes a painful throat with difficulty swallowing. The patient may very well have a fever due to the inflammation, and when the doctor looks at the back of the throat, he or she will see redness, swelling, and sometimes some pus. Hopefully these infections are mild and readily treatable. However, if any infection is severe and spreads throughout the entire body,

Because of their abnormal immune systems, lupus patients must wash their hands many times a day to help prevent major infections, which can be life-threatening. **(Mark Burnett/Alamy)**

or severely injures a major organ (such as the lung from pneumonia), it could potentially be deadly.

So how can you prevent these infections from occurring in the first place? The most important thing is to take care of your lupus using all the therapies that keep it under control. Some of the therapies for lupus do not suppress the immune system at all and can help to decrease the need for higher doses of the stronger medicines which do suppress the immune system. All patients with SLE should be taking Plaquenil (hydroxychloroquine) daily as long as they are not allergic to it. This medicine is by far the safest drug to treat SLE. It doesn't suppress the immune system, and it can help decrease the need for stronger medicines. All patients should also be using sunscreen on all exposed body areas every day because ultraviolet (UV) light increases lupus activity. Even if they don't go outside, this should be done, as even indoor lighting has UV activity. On sunny days, sunscreen should be reapplied several times throughout the day if one goes outside at all. Patients should not smoke cigarettes for several reasons. Smoking decreases the effectiveness of Plaquenil, basically counteracting its effects which could potentially cause your doctor to have to use stronger immune suppressing medicines. In addition, smoking itself can actually cause lupus to flare up due to a chemical called hydrazine which is contained in the cigarette. Patients should also get 8 hours of sleep each night, try to decrease their daily stress levels, eat a well-balanced diet, and exercise regularly. All of these things will improve their health and their immune function.

Vaccinations can prevent certain infections from occurring. All patients should get a vaccination to prevent pneumonia called Pneumovax. It should be given at least twice, 5 years apart. This vaccine is to prevent infections from pneumococcus which is the most common bacteria causing pneumonia. Pneumonia is the most common cause of infection death in patients with SLE. An influenza vaccine, commonly called the "flu shot," should be administered every fall. Influenza kills 30,000 Americans every year. The vast majority of those who die are the elderly, the very young, and the immunosuppressed (like patients with SLE). An important thing to note is that the "flu shot" never gives anyone the flu. This is unfortunately a common, incorrect belief that keeps many people from getting it. Patients should also get a diphtheria/tetanus booster shot every 10 years.

A new, emerging problem is the H1N1 influenza, also called swine flu. At the time of my writing this article (September 2009), a vaccine is being studied for use to prevent H1N1. The Centers for Disease Control [and Prevention]at this time recommends that patients with SLE who are 6 months to 64 years of age receive the vaccine. Those who are 65 years and older should get it if there is additional vaccine available after other target groups are treated first (such as pregnant women, household contacts of children less than 6 months old, and everyone between the ages of 6 months and 24 years old).

> **FAST FACT**
>
> Both bacterial and viral infections can cause symptoms such as malaise, fever, and chills. Viral infections, however, cannot be cured by antibiotics.

Some special vaccines should be considered in certain circumstances. If an SLE patient has a household member who has chronic hepatitis B infection, he or she should get the hepatitis B vaccine, which is done as a three-part series. Patients who have had their spleen removed (sometimes done for severe low blood count problems) should receive the meningococcal vaccine.

It is very important to keep in mind that SLE patients who are on immunosuppressant medicines to treat their lupus, therefore making it more difficult to fight off infections, should not receive vaccines which have live organisms as part of the vaccine. The medications that can suppress the immune system include prednisone at more than 7.5 mg a day, methotrexate, Arava (leflunomide), Imuran (azathioprine), CellCept (mycophenolate), Cytoxan (cyclophosphamide),

Humira (adalimumab), Enbrel (etanercept), Simponi (golimumab), Cimzia (Certolizumab pegol), Remicade (infliximab), and Rituxan (rituximab). The live virus vaccines which need to be avoided include MMR (measles, mumps, and rubella), OPV (polio), BCG, vaccinia, typhoid, yellow fever, FluMist (nasal flu vaccine), and the new vaccine to prevent shingles, Zostavax. The previously mentioned vaccines (Pneumovax, influenza "flu shot", diphtheria/tetanus booster, hepatitis B, and meningococcal vaccine) are not live vaccines and can be used safely by all patients.

A special note needs to be made regarding patients who are going to be placed on the medicine rituximab (Rituxan). This medicine blunts the effects of vaccines. Therefore, if one is going to be placed on Rituxan, one should make sure they get any vaccines that they need before they get the Rituxan. If they are already being treated with Rituxan, they should discuss with their rheumatologist about when the best timing for their vaccines should be done.

Patients 60 years of age or older who have never had a varicella vaccination and who are not on these immunosuppressant medicines should strongly consider getting the Zostavax vaccine. This vaccination helps to prevent shingles, a very painful rash which is due to the chicken pox virus and occurs in around 20% of SLE patients at some point.

If you have any family or friends who get a live vaccine listed above, it is important to realize that you could potentially get infected from them after they get the vaccine if you are immunosuppressed. So if you are on any of the above-listed immunosuppressant medications, and a close contact receives any of the above listed live vaccines, you should avoid contact with them for 2 weeks. If they get the OPV for polio, you should avoid contact for 4 weeks. A better alternative than the OPV would be for them to instead get vaccinated with eIPV, which does not contain any live polio virus, and therefore you wouldn't have to avoid them.

Another important point is that none of these vaccines are 100% effective. In other words, you can still get the infection after you get the vaccine. However, getting these vaccines helps to keep the infection less severe compared to if you did not get the vaccine in the first place.

It is also important to not get any vaccination while your lupus is very active, as vaccines can sometimes cause lupus flares to worsen. You should also probably not get a vaccine while on 40mg of prednisone a day or more, as you are less likely to respond to the vaccine. You should always ask your rheumatologist whether it is safe to get any vaccine before you do so.

Another preventable infection is endocarditis, which is an infection of the heart valves. This can happen to anyone with an abnormal heart valve who has dental work done. Approximately 10% of lupus patients have abnormal heart valves. When dental work is performed, a large amount of bacteria enters the blood stream and can land on and infect a damaged heart valve. This type of infection can be deadly, but if antibiotics are taken, it can be prevented. Heart valve abnormalities are diagnosed by a special type of ultrasound of the heart, called an echocardiogram. Any patient with SLE who has a heart murmur (an abnormal heart sound on physical examination) or who is positive for antiphospholipid antibodies (which include anticardiolipin antibodies, lupus anticoagulant, false positive syphilis test, and anti beta 2-glycoprotein I antibodies) should have an echocardiogram to make sure they don't have a heart valve problem. If they do, then they should take antibiotics before and after dental procedures.

A commonly missed form of infection prevention is to avoid hand contact, sneezing, and coughing from infected persons. Avoiding those who are sick and frequently washing your hands are important, especially during cold and flu season.

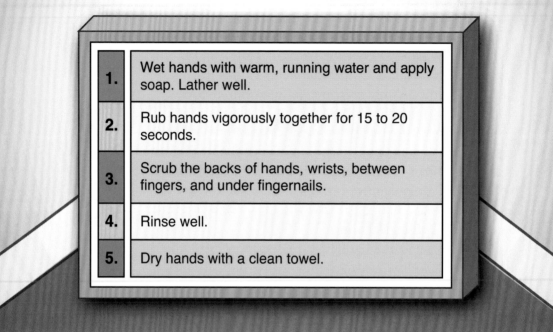

How to Wash Hands to Help Prevent Common Infections

1.	Wet hands with warm, running water and apply soap. Lather well.
2.	Rub hands vigorously together for 15 to 20 seconds.
3.	Scrub the backs of hands, wrists, between fingers, and under fingernails.
4.	Rinse well.
5.	Dry hands with a clean towel.

All SLE patients should call and see their physician immediately if they have any infection symptoms. These especially include fevers and body chills. Although fever can happen due to lupus itself, this should never be assumed, as infection can do the same thing, and the treatment is different than what is used to treat lupus itself. Other symptoms of an infection can depend upon the area in which they are occurring, for example: headache and congestion for sinusitis, coughing up sputum in pneumonia, painful and frequent urination with a urinary tract infection, and warm tender skin with a skin infection (cellulitis). Infections should be assessed and treated by your primary care physician, usually an internal medicine or family medicine physician. If it is after-hours, a weekend, or your doctor is not available, you may be directed to go to your local emergency room. Although an ER [emergency room] visit can end up being a long affair, it is very important to do this, as a potential infection could be very dangerous if not diagnosed and treated promptly. Your primary care physician may also ask you to call and see your rheumatologist if there is the possibility that your lupus may be the cause of your symptoms. Sometimes it can be difficult to figure out if the symptoms are due to lupus or infection, and you may need to be treated for the possibility of both conditions.

There are some other common infections to look out for. If white patches occur in the mouth, or if you have a dry mouth and your tongue becomes sore and red, these may be signs of a yeast infection due to a yeast called *Candida albicans*. This infection is called thrush and is treated with antifungal medicines. If you develop a burning, uncomfortable red rash on one side of the body, oftentimes associated with small blisters, this could be shingles (due to chicken pox virus, varicella) and should be treated with antiviral medicines.

An important thing to also remember is that not all infections are treatable. For example, infections due to some viruses, such as viral sinus infections, bronchitis, and colds, do not respond to any antibiotics at all. Your doctor may not recommend any treatment except over-the-counter medicines to help you feel better. This is very important, because too many patients are inappropriately given antibiotics too often, and this can lead to organisms becoming resistant to our antibiotics, making them much more difficult to treat. Taking Vitamin C and Echinacea (an herb from the purple coneflower) has not been shown to be effective for the common cold. In fact, patients with SLE should not take Echinacea as it could potentially make lupus worse. One possible treatment for the common cold is to use over-the-counter zinc lozenges, which have been shown to possibly decrease the duration of symptoms of the infection.

If offered antibiotics, SLE patients need to remember that they should always list sulfa antibiotics as one of their allergies, even if they have never taken one before. Sulfa antibiotics such as Septra, Bactrim, trimethoprim-sulfamethoxizole, Gantrisin, and sulfadiazine can cause lupus to flare up, and lupus patients have a high chance of being allergic to them as well.

In summary, infections are unfortunately a common reason that some SLE patients don't do well. However, the chances of having a bad infection can be minimized by being compliant with using your Plaquenil and sunscreen daily, not smoking, living a healthy lifestyle, and making sure vaccinations are kept up-to-date. Any infection symptoms should also be evaluated and treated by a healthcare professional as soon as possible. These measures are important keys to living with lupus successfully.

Lupus Can Cause Both Psychiatric and Neurological Problems

Nicholas A. Doninger, Tammy O. Utset, and Joseph W. Fink

Nicholas A. Doninger is an assistant professor of psychiatry at Wright State University and a clinical neuropsychologist at Kettering Medical Center; Tammy O. Utset is an associate professor of medicine at the University of Chicago; and Joseph W. Fink is an assistant professor of clinical psychiatry at the University of Chicago. In this viewpoint the team of researchers describes how lupus can cause a number of psychiatric problems for patients, including depression, anxiety, and sometimes psychosis. Psychiatric symptoms occur for as many as 60 percent of lupus patients. They can be caused by the life changes necessitated by the various effects of lupus or by the medicines used to treat the disorder. In addition to psychiatric symptoms, neurological problems such as deficits in learning, memory, information processing, and more can also occur in lupus patients. While psychiatric issues can be treated with drugs, no therapies are available to treat the negative neurocognitive effects of lupus.

Individuals with lupus can develop a variety of psychiatric problems, which can aggravate other symptoms. Although these problems generally do not differ in nature from individuals with other types of chronic diseases, it remains unclear whether psychiatric symptoms reflect the effects of disease activity on the brain (e.g., immunological response), misattributions or a stressful reaction to physical disabilities and psychosocial dysfunction. The most common psychiatric problems experienced by individuals with lupus include depression, anxiety and, rarely, psychosis.

Clinical depression is a disabling, unpleasant and prolonged mood associated with a variety of symptoms: sadness, sleep and appetite changes, irritability, guilty feelings, lowered self-esteem, inability to concentrate, lack of interest in enjoyable activities, and suicidal thoughts. Physical features may include headaches, body aches and pains, constipation or diarrhea, and fatigue. People who suffer with clinical depression do not necessarily experience all of these symptoms. Anxiety disorders develop when worry and fear become persistent and overwhelming and start to interfere with daily life. An often-overlooked symptom in SLE is anxiety attacks, or "panic attacks," which are a sudden, unrealistic sense of impending doom, which occurs for no apparent reason.

Lupus psychosis refers to a severe mental disturbance marked by difficulty judging reality, organizing thoughts, and/or hallucinations (sounds or sights). It is believed to be due to the direct effects of lupus on the brain. Although the symptoms may resemble schizophrenia, in lupus they generally are not chronic in nature (i.e., the symptoms go away over time with treatment for active lupus). Fortunately this type of psychiatric problem is the least commonly observed in lupus patients. Physicians are becoming increasingly aware of these problems and are making these diagnoses with more frequency. . . . Often a psychiatric consultation may be helpful in clarifying the diagnosis and starting appropriate treatment(s).

Psychiatric Problems in Lupus

The frequency of psychiatric symptoms is estimated to be as high as 60%. Psychiatric symptoms typically occur early in the illness and may predate the diagnosis by as much as a year. Although infrequent, psychosis is now used by doctors as a hallmark criterion for the diagnosis of systemic lupus. Depression and anxiety often go unrecognized among those with medical illnesses because symptoms such as lethargy, loss of interest, and insomnia resemble those associated with the underlying medical condition. The common notion that those with a chronic illness should feel depressed "because they are sick" may needlessly contribute to the undertreatment of patients who respond well to standard treatments.

Lupus can cause psychiatric problems for patients, including anxiety and depression and, rarely, psychosis. (L. Williams/Photo Researchers, Inc.)

The causes of clinical depression in lupus remain a topic of controversy. Individuals with lupus can become depressed as a result of making continuous life adjustments and the negative impact of the disease on self-image and functional capacity. Alternatively, the disease can cause symptoms of depression through the effect of autoimmune processes on the brain and other organ systems such as the heart and kidneys. Medications used to treat lupus such as steroids, may also induce mood changes. Panic attacks are thought to be due to over activity of the brain's sympathetic nervous system releasing large amounts of adrenalin, which causes a racing heart, rapid breathing, sweating, and trembling.

Most psychotic episodes occur when lupus targets the brain, e.g., vasculitis (inflammation of blood vessels). Although uncommon, psychosis may emerge as a toxic side effect of steroid medications such as prednisone. Other rare causes of psychosis include hyponatremia (or low blood levels of sodium), seizures, hyperventilation, or antimalarial therapy.

The Treatment and Prognosis for Psychiatric Problems in Lupus

Depression

Treating and managing depression in lupus requires a comprehensive approach. Any underlying medical factors contributing to the depression must be identified and addressed. Antidepressant medications are often used and can be very helpful in improving the patient's outlook and level of function.

Selective Serotonin Re-uptake Inhibitors (SSRIs) [a class of compounds often used as antidepressants] have more favorable side effect profiles and work more quickly than the older tricyclic antidepressants; however, tricyclics [a class of antidepressant drugs] may still be used when sleep disturbance is a prominent feature. For those who are unable to tolerate SSRIs, venlafaxine and Moclobemide may be suitable. Psychotherapy can also be helpful in assisting people to understand relationships between their feelings and illness, and coping more effectively with daily stress and life adjustments. Effective treatment also involves the cooperation of the patient, and the support, education, and involvement of the patient's family and close friends. Unfortunately, depression can recur so it is important to recognize the signs and symptoms so that treatment can be started as quickly as possible.

Anxiety

Laboratory tests and a physical examination may be useful in detecting medical conditions, which could be contributing to anxiety. Treatments used in anxiety disorders include cognitive behavioral therapy (CBT), exposure, anxiety management, relaxation techniques, and lifestyle changes. In CBT, individuals learn to cope with situations or physical sensations that cause distress through gradual and controlled exposure to them. In addition, unproductive or harmful thoughts, which may contribute to anxious feelings are targeted. The individual critically examines the logic underlying their feelings and learns to develop more adaptive ways to appraise the source of their distress. Relaxation techniques, including breathing retraining and meditation may also be added to help develop skills in coping more effectively with the physical symptoms of anxiety.

> **FAST FACT**
>
> Lupus strikes adult women ten to fifteen times more frequently than adult men.

Drugs used to treat anxiety disorders include the SSRIs and tricyclics, benzodiazepines [depressant medication], beta-blockers [medications that reduce blood pressure], and monoamine oxidase inhibitors [antidepressants]. Each of these treatments is effective and may be offered alone or in combination.

Changes in lifestyle, including exercise and diet, can also help improve the symptoms of anxiety. In particular, a program of regular exercise can: 1) reduce muscle tension, 2) lower the level of adrenalin (the substance responsible for feelings of arousal), and 3) discharge pent-up frustrations, which can aggravate panic reactions. Dietary modifications can also have a direct impact on the body's internal physiology. In particular, the elimination of caffeine and nicotine may be critical for reducing anxiety and panic attacks.

Lupus Psychosis

The symptoms of psychosis are typically treated with antipsychotic medications, high doses of cortisone-related (steroid) medications, such as prednisone or prednisolone, and sometimes powerful immune suppression drugs, such as cyclophosphamide (Cytoxan).

Neurocognitive Disturbances with Lupus

Neurocognitive dysfunction is also a common and overlooked clinical feature of lupus estimated to occur in up to 80% of affected individuals. The diversity of cognitive impairments parallels the considerable variability of the disease process. Deficits in learning and/or memory, reasoning, verbal fluency, motor function, basic attention, and information processing speed are the most consistently described. These deficits have been characterized as generally mild to moderate in severity, fluctuating over time, and non-progressive in nature; however, recent research has associated a higher risk for progression of cognitive impairments with the presence of certain disease activity markers. . . .

In general, objective tests of cognitive performance are unrelated to perceived stress, depression, and anxiety, suggesting that cognitive impairment may be a primary disease manifestation consistent with other immune-mediated disease [conditions resulting from an abnormal immune system] with neurologic involvement (e.g., acquired immune deficiency syndrome and multiple sclerosis). Alternatively, the relationship between depression and cognitive performance may be determined by more subtle aspects of lupus, including sleep disturbance, fatigue, and pain as has been suggested in studies of individuals with multiple sclerosis. Neuropsychological assessment with a qualified neuropsychologist is useful in delineating cognitive strengths and weakness, including the extent to which clinical factors such as depression may be moderating cognitive performance, which can ultimately contribute to effective treatment planning.

Currently, there is no specific therapy which improves chronic neurocognitive impairment from lupus, and interventions focus on adaptive strategies to

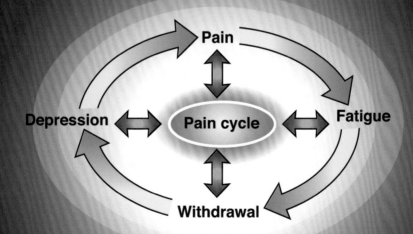

Pain and Psychiatric Response

Chronic pain sufferers, such as those with lupus, may develop a pain cycle in which physical pain may lead to or feed off of feelings of depression, fatigue, and withdrawal.

Pain

Depression ⟷ Pain cycle ⟷ Fatigue

Withdrawal

Taken from: Virtual Health Care Team, "Systemic Lupus Erythematosus,"
www.vhct.org/case2700/images/pain_cycle.jpg, 2006.

compensate for areas of cognitive weakness. If impairments are due to depression, treating the depression can improve brain function. Lupus neurocognitive impairment is an area of intense research which may yield therapeutic interventions in the future. Thus, it is reasonable to identify the problem and track it over time if patients have substantial difficulties with memory, concentration or other mental function.

Advances in Lupus Research and Treatment

Lupus Foundation of America

The Lupus Foundation of America Inc. (LFA) is the foremost national nonprofit voluntary health organization dedicated to finding the causes of and cure for lupus. The foundation provides support and services to all people affected by lupus. In this article the foundation reports that new advances in lupus treatment give hope to the 1.5 million Americans living with the disease. Both public and private support for lupus research has increased, and a new public education campaign was launched in 2009. In addition to these advances, the LFA released a list of ten important advances made in lupus research in 2008 alone. These advances have been made in the areas of genetic research, drug treatment data, congressional spending, and more.

[In January 2009] the Lupus Foundation of America, Inc. (LFA) [reported that] continuing progress was achieved in 2008 in efforts to combat lupus, a chronic autoimmune disease which affects an

SOURCE: Lupus Foundation of America, "2008 Was a Year of Progress and Hope for a Better Quality of Life for 1.5 Million Americans Affected by Lupus," www.lupus.org, January 26, 2009. Reproduced by permission.

estimated 1.5 million Americans and at least five million people worldwide. Teams of researchers announced important findings which provided clues to the underlying genetic origins of lupus, several companies released clinical data on studies of potential new treatments, and Congress reaffirmed its commitment to provide greatly expanded federal support for lupus research and education programs.

Multiple studies provided insight into new ways to manage and treat lupus, and prevent its often-devastating consequences. National media coverage of lupus continued to rise, and . . . work neared completion on the first-ever Advertising Council national lupus public education campaign, scheduled to launch in early 2009.

Public and Private Support for Lupus Research and Education Grows

The largest sources of funding for lupus research are the federal government and the pharmaceutical and biotechnology industries. In 2008, the LFA worked with elected officials and industry leaders to further expand investment in research on lupus, while the Foundation expanded the scope of its own lupus research program.

Congress appropriated millions of dollars in FY [fiscal year] 2009 for lupus research and education programs funded through the Department of Health and Human Services, National Institutes of Health, Centers for Disease Control and Prevention, and Office on Women's Health, and the Department of Defense's Peer Reviewed Medical Research Program.

Private funding for lupus research also grew in 2008, as evidenced by the growing number of clinical research studies to test potential new, safe and effective treatments for lupus by pharmaceutical and biotechnology companies. Several companies announced preliminary data from their clinical studies. While some trials did not reach targeted endpoints, data gathered from these stud-

Strategy to Fund Research Is a Success

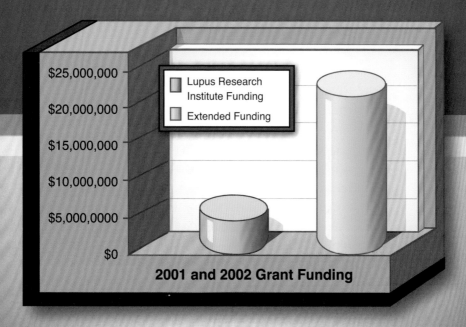

Lupus Research Institute $6 Million Investment Yields $23 Million in Government and Other Funding

- Lupus Research Institute Funding
- Extended Funding

$25,000,000
$20,000,000
$15,000,000
$10,000,000
$5,000,0000
$0

2001 and 2002 Grant Funding

Taken from: Lupus Research Institute, "LRI Strategy to Fund Novel Research Is Stellar Success," January 30, 2007. www.lupusresearchinstitute.org.

ies provide insight into possible new ways to design clinical trials and select patients for studies.

The Lupus Foundation of America (LFA) in 2008 provided another $1.1 million to support its own national research program, "Bringing Down the Barriers." To date, the LFA and its chapters have provided more than $20 million to support approximately 400 investigators at 100 academic and scientific institutions. The LFA has greatly expanded the scope of its program to support research initiatives in novel pilot approaches, pediatric/adolescent lupus, lupus in males, mid-to-late stage translational research, and studies on the use of adult stem cells in lupus.

Although a number of scientific challenges lay ahead, developments in 2008 brought renewed hope that a better quality of life for people with lupus and their families is possible within the not too distant future.

The LFA has compiled a list of ten important advances in lupus research and education that occurred during 2008. They are as follows:

Researchers Identify Genes Linked to the Underlying Causes of Lupus

International teams of investigators identified four new genes that are strongly associated with lupus, and ten others that are possible risk factors. A second research team identified regions on two chromosomes that may contribute to individuals being predisposed to lupus. The findings may one day make it possible to identify who may be at risk for lupus and prevent its consequences.

Congress Provides Millions of Dollars for Lupus Research and Education

The U.S. Congress provided another $3.1 million to fund lupus epidemiological research through the Centers for Disease Control and Prevention (CDC) for the National Lupus Patient Registry. Congress also authorized funds to support studies on lupus and lupus biomarkers through the Department of Defense Peer Reviewed Medical Research Program. This initiative has provided more than $6 million for lupus research. Additionally, Congress provided funding for the National Institutes of Health (NIH), which provided an estimated $84 million for lupus research in 2008.

Industry Expands Efforts on Drug Development Providing Hope for Better Quality of Life

Biotechnology and pharmaceutical companies stepped up efforts in 2008 to develop new treatments for lupus, with several releasing data on clinical studies of potential new treatments. Companies working to develop new therapies for lupus include Amgen, Bristol-Myers Squibb, Dynavax/Galxo-SmithKline, Genelabs Technologies, Genentech/Biogen Idec, Hoffmann-La Roche, Human Genome Sciences/Glaxo-SmithKline, La Jolla Pharmaceutical Company/BioMarin, MedImmune/AstraZeneca, Merck Serono, Roche Pharmaceuticals, UCB, Vifor Pharma/Aspreva Pharmaceuticals, and Wyeth Pharmaceuticals.

LFA Establishes the Michael Jon Barlin Pediatric Research Program to Address Specialized Issues Related to Lupus in Children and Expands the Scope of Its Lupus Research Program

In 2008, the LFA became the only national voluntary health organization with a research program specifically dedicated to studies on lupus in children when it launched the Michael Jon Barlin Pediatric Research Program. The LFA awarded $1.1 million in research grants and fellowships last year to advance the science of lupus by supporting studies in novel pilot approaches, pediatric/adolescent lupus, lupus in males, and mid-to-late stage translational research. Additionally, LFA supported studies on stem cell research, cutaneous (skin) lupus, kidney disease and lupus, and the neuropsychiatric effects of lupus, and awarded five student summer fellowships to foster an interest in the field of lupus research.

FAST FACT

As of 2008 the Alliance for Lupus Research had committed $50 million to lupus research, making the organization the largest private source of funds for lupus research in the world.

Study Data Provides Evidence of New Benefits for Existing Lupus Treatments

Clinical research data released in 2008 showed that lupus patients treated with hydroxychloroquine, used most often to treat lupus skin and joint problems, were less likely to have kidney disease, had less severe disease and required lower doses of corticosteroids than patients who did not receive the drug. Another study showed that two therapies, mycophenolate mofetil (MMF) and intravenous cyclophosphamide (IV CYC) appeared to be safe and effective for treatment of lupus nephritis (LN) in adolescents.

Studies Provide Hope and Tools for Successful Lupus Pregnancies

Researchers found a relationship between the levels of a protein called sFlt-1 and preeclampsia in pregnant women with lupus, allowing for earlier management and monitoring by specialists in high-risk obstetric care. Preeclampsia is characterized by high blood pressure and large losses of protein in the urine and is dangerous for both the mother and the baby. Another study found intravenous immunoglobulin infusion (IVIg) to be safe

To increase public awareness of lupus—and to help fund research into the disease—celebrities dressed as "Hollywood bag ladies" auction off their handbags.
(AP Images)

and effective for women with lupus who had consecutive miscarriages.

Second International Conference on Lupus Flares Addresses Gaps in Clinical Research

More than 80 international scientific thought leaders in lupus continued their work in 2008 to address an important gap impeding lupus drug development and approval during the Second International Conference on Lupus Flares organized by the LFA. Experts discussed modifications to tools used to monitor disease activity and progression. They also worked to finalize a consensus definition of a lupus flare. The number of flares and time to flare can be used as primary endpoints in clinical studies; however, presently there is no accepted definition of a lupus flare.

LFA Launches Center for Clinical Trials Education (CCTE) to Educate People Interested in Lupus Clinical Studies

The LFA launched the Center for Clinical Trials Education (CCTE) as a resource for people with lupus and their families who are considering participation in a clinical trial. The CCTE website serves as a national clearing house of information specific to lupus clinical trials and volunteer participation. The website includes a lupus trial-locating service and provides information about clinical trials in English and Spanish tailored to various populations of people with lupus.

Lupus Advocates Generate Increased Attention and Resources for Research and Education Programs

More than 300 individuals with lupus, their families, and health professionals from 37 states came to Washington as part of the LFA's Tenth Annual Advocacy Day and met with 200 Members of the United States Congress and staff members. In 2008, Congress provided support for legislative priorities advocated by the LFA, including expanded funding for lupus research and education programs.

Public Awareness Initiatives Improve Understanding of Lupus and Its Impact on Individuals and Families

The LFA was named the Founding Partner with the U.S. Department of Health and Human Services Office on Women's Health (OWH) on the first-ever Advertising Council national lupus public awareness campaign, which is scheduled to launch in early 2009, reach an estimated 100 million U.S. adults, and generate $30–$50 million annually in free media exposure for lupus. Media coverage for lupus in 2008 included a feature on lupus as part of a week-long series about chronic diseases broadcast on *NBC Nightly News*. *ABC News Now*, CNN, and Accent Health also produced feature reports on lupus.

CHAPTER 2

Perspectives into Lupus

Men with Lupus Face Unique Challenges

Lupus Foundation of America

The Lupus Foundation of America Inc. (LFA) is the foremost national nonprofit voluntary health organization dedicated to finding the cause of and cure for lupus. The foundation provides support and services to all people affected by lupus. In this viewpoint the foundation explains that although nine out of ten lupus patients are women, men also suffer from the disease. Men with lupus are likely to have less of the male sex hormone androgen, but this does not make them less masculine than other men. There are some clinical differences between men and women with lupus. For example, kidney disease and kidney failure are more common for men. Unlike women with the disorder, men are also more likely to feel stigmatized for having what is generally considered a "woman's disease."

Photo on previous page. Linda Gomez, of Montgomery, Alabama, started an online lupus support group in 2009. Many such sites have begun to appear on the Internet. **(AP Images)**

Systemic lupus erythematosus [SLE] is a very challenging disease. Although some features of lupus are common, such as joint pain and fatigue, lupus is different in every person. It is truly a disease that seemingly provokes more questions than it provides answers.

SOURCE: Lupus Foundation of America, "How Lupus Differs in Men," www.lupus.org. Reproduced by permission.

While the pathogenesis, or reasons for development, of lupus remains unknown, genetic, environmental, and hormonal factors certainly play a role. Most people think of lupus as a disease of women of childbearing age—and with good reason: 90% of lupus patients between the ages of 15 and 45 are women. However, after the age of 50 (approximately the age of the onset of menopause)

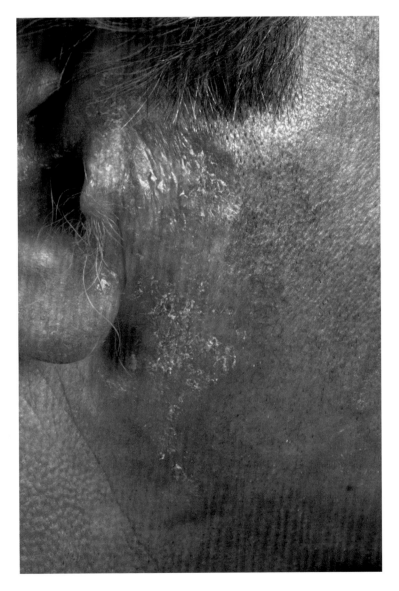

Men with lupus are sometimes reluctant to admit they have the illness, fearing they may be stigmatized for having what is often considered a woman's disease. (**Biophoto Associates/Photo Researchers, Inc.**)

the percentage of women with lupus falls to 75% and the percentage of men with the disease rises to 25%. Therefore it is a mistake to think of lupus as exclusively a women's health concern.

Role of Sex Hormones

The role of sex hormones in the development and clinical expression of lupus is complex. For instance, flares in women may be influenced by their hormonal status; one example is that pregnancy can trigger a flare.

Simply put, two broad types of sex hormones exist. Estrogens are typically considered the "female hormones," and androgens are considered to be the "male hormones." Both types are produced in both sexes. However, estrogens—in addition to their role in the development of secondary sex characteristics (i.e., facial hair in males or breast development in females)—may encourage autoimmune disorders, while androgens may be protective instead.

Some studies have noted lower levels of a specific androgen, testosterone, in some men with lupus. Men with lupus, however, are in no way less masculine than men without lupus, and sexual activity, potency, and fertility in men with lupus does not differ from men without lupus.

Clinical Similarities and Differences

Several studies have tried to characterize lupus in men, in particular searching for any clinical differences between men and women. The results of these studies are difficult to interpret for several reasons: the small number of male patients, differences in study methods, ethnic and racial differences that may influence the way lupus affects certain individuals. The accompanying table summarizes clinical differences found in some of the most frequently quoted studies. . . .

Reported Clinical Differences in Male and Female Lupus Patients

Study	Features More Common in Men	Features More Common in Women
1. M.H. Miller et al. (1983)	Pleurisy (inflammation of the sac around the lungs)	Neurologic (nervous system) symptoms Alopecia (hair loss) Thrombocytopenia (abnormal decrease in blood platelets)
2. L.D. Kaufman et al. (1989)	Renal (kidney) disease Thrombocytopenia	- - -
3. M.M. Ward and S. Studenski (1990)	Renal failure Seizures	- - -
4. J. Font et al. (1992)	Discoid lupus (reddish, scaly skin) Subacute cutaneous lupus (skin lesions)	Malar rash (rash on cheeks) Arthritis
5. M. Petri (1997)	Hemolytic anemia (from the destruction of red blood cells) Lupus anticoagulant (can promote abnormal blood clotting) Seizures	Sjogren's syndrome (glandular damage that causes dryness of eyes and mouth)

Taken from: www.lupus.org.

A study by Dr. Michelle Petri from Johns Hopkins University tried to address the differences in men and women lupus patients by comparing the clinical and laboratory features of a group of 41 males and 545 females. She found that men had an increased frequency of seizures, immune-mediated anemia, and lupus anticoagulant (which may lead to clotting problems), but a lower frequency of Sjögren's disease. Her study suggests that men may have more severe disease than women.

Even though the percentages of certain symptoms may be different in men and women, the manifestations are very similar. For example, the arthritis of lupus, which typically affects the small joints of the hands and is associated with morning stiffness, is the same in men and women. And, while the frequency of discoid lupus erythematosus (DLE) may be more common in males, the characteristic flat, non-painful, scarring lesions look identical in both sexes. The same is true for the acute rashes (malar rash) and for subacute cutaneous lupus erythematosus (SCLE).

Drug-induced lupus erythematosus (DILE) illustrates the role of environmental triggers in the development of lupus. DILE is commonly associated with [the drugs] hydralazine, procainamide, and isoniazid, and is more common in men because the disorders for which some of these medications are used (e.g., high blood pressure, irregular heart rhythms) are diagnosed more often in men.

As our understanding of lupus increases, additional research is needed to identify subsets of people with lupus in order to improve the treatments and outcomes of those patients.

Coping with Lupus

Anyone, male or female, who has been diagnosed with lupus has experienced the frustration of uncertainty and the difficulty of learning the new language needed to understand this disease. Anxiety about the future as well as family and employment issues are common concerns.

Men with lupus face a unique challenge. It may be difficult for them to discuss a disease that so many people think occurs only in women. Because there are fewer

FAST FACT

Twenty percent of people with lupus have a parent or sibling who has lupus.

men with systemic lupus, they may have trouble meeting other men with the disease. This may prevent them from gaining the benefits of mutual support. While many of our female patients are interested in meeting any other people with lupus, virtually all of our male patients ask about other men with whom they can speak.

Current research may provide new insights into the immune system and the role that genetic and hormonal factors play in autoimmune diseases. Variables related to gender may help unravel the mysteries of lupus, but it is impossible to predict a person's progress based on gender alone. And, it is important to remember that the management of lupus is tailored to the clinical manifestations of each individual.

Health Risks Are High for Pregnant Women with Lupus

Medical News Today

Medical News Today is the largest independent health and medical news Web site on the Internet. The Web site reports that women who have lupus can have healthy pregnancies, but they do face a more than twentyfold greater risk of death during labor than women without lupus. Women with lupus are also more likely to suffer from complications in pregnancy and much more likely to deliver via cesarean section than other women. Because of these risks, vigilant medical care is necessary for pregnant lupus patients.

Women with systemic lupus who become pregnant are at significantly greater risk for death or other medical complications than are pregnant women without lupus, Duke University Medical Center researchers have found in a nationwide study of more than 18 million women.

SOURCE: DukeHealth.org, "Pregnant Women with Lupus Face Higher Risk of Complications and Death," November 15, 2006. Reproduced by permission.

The study, believed to be the largest of its kind, suggests that pregnant women with systemic lupus should be considered a high-risk population and should be monitored closely by both a rheumatologist and an obstetrician who specializes in caring for high-risk patients, the researchers said.

"Pregnant women with lupus should never try to go through their pregnancy alone and simply hope for the best," said study leader Megan Clowse, M.D., M.P.H., assistant professor in the Division of Rheumatology. "They should stay in close contact with their doctors and report any problems immediately."

Clowse presented the findings on Sunday, Nov. 12 [2006] at the annual meeting of the American College of Rheumatology, in Washington, D.C. The study was funded by the National Institutes of Health's Building Interdisciplinary Research Careers in Women's Health program.

> **FAST FACT**
>
> Only about 5 percent of children born to individuals with lupus will develop the disease.

Lupus is an autoimmune disease in which the immune system loses its ability to distinguish between "self" and foreign substances and thus relentlessly attacks the body's own tissues and cells. Individuals with lupus often exhibit many different symptoms, including arthritis, kidney disease, rashes, fevers, anemia and sensitivity to light, among other problems.

Approximately 1.5 million Americans—roughly 90 percent of them women—have some type of lupus. Most patients are diagnosed during their reproductive years. Seventy percent of patients have systemic lupus, the most severe form of the disease.

All women with systemic lupus, pregnant or not, are at increased risk for death and medical complications compared to a healthy population, Clowse said. Other studies report that each year, between 0.8 percent and 3 percent of lupus patients die from the disease.

Pregnant Women with Lupus Are More Likely to Die in Labor

Previous research also has shown that pregnancy can increase the activity level of lupus, increasing the danger to the woman and sometimes causing problems in her fetus, according to Clowse. What was not certain, she said, is how much lupus increased a woman's health risk.

To help answer this question, Clowse's team analyzed data from more than 18 million pregnancy-related hospital admissions and discharges in the United States from 2000 to 2002. The study found that slightly more than 13,500 women with systemic lupus gave birth during this time, and 44 of the women—0.3 percent—died, Clowse said.

Overall, women with systemic lupus showed a more than 20-fold greater risk of pregnancy-related death,

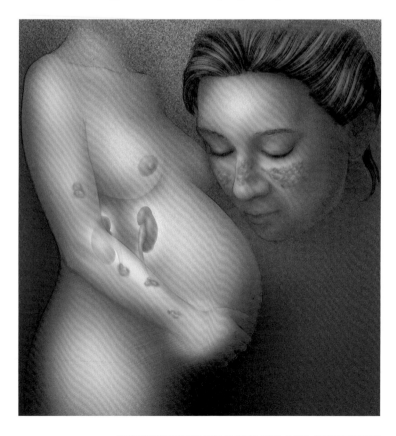

Recent studies have found that women with systemic lupus erythematosus have twenty times the risk of pregnancy-related death than women not having the disease. (Brian Evans/Photo Researchers, Inc.)

compared with women without the disease, she said. Extrapolating this observed increase in risk to the general population suggests that for every 100,000 women with systemic lupus who would deliver a baby, approximately 325 of them would die, compared with approximately 14 deaths for every 100,000 women without the disease who would give birth, Clowse said.

"We don't want these results to scare women with lupus away from getting pregnant, especially if they have a mild form of the disease," Clowse said. "But these women really must plan their pregnancies. They may need to change their medications before they get pregnant, and they really shouldn't conceive when their lupus is active."

Clowse said patients whose lupus has been dormant for at least six months before conception are at low risk for developing active systemic lupus during pregnancy and therefore are at least somewhat less likely than women whose disease is active to experience health complications.

Lupus and Complications in Pregnancy

However, all women with systemic lupus do face elevated risks for pregnancy complications, she said. In the study population, women with systemic lupus, compared to women without the disease, were nearly six times more likely to suffer from deep vein thrombosis—a blood clot—and 3.5 times more likely to develop sepsis, a severe illness caused by an extreme infection of the bloodstream. Many women with lupus also were anemic or had low blood platelet counts at delivery and were three times more likely to need transfusions.

Additionally, almost 37 percent of women with lupus gave birth via cesarean section—15 percent higher than the national average of 22 percent. Women with lupus also were 2.5 times more likely to experience preterm labor and three times more likely to develop preeclampsia, or pregnancy-related high blood pressure, than women without lupus. Clowse said the study's results are highly

Health Risks for Pregnant Women with Lupus

According to a 2006 study by the American College of Rheumatology, compared with pregnant women without the disease, women with lupus are:

- More likely to have coexisting disease including diabetes, kidney failure, and hypertension.

- More likely to experience a blood clot, stroke, or develop a life-threatening infection.

- More likely to have low platelet counts and anemia during delivery, which may contribute to their threefold increased need for transfusion during pregnancy.

Taken from: Denise Mann, "Risks for Pregnant Women with Lupus," November 14, 2006.
http://lupus.webmd.com/news/20061115/women-with-lupus-pregnancy-risks.

suggestive and should be taken seriously within the health care community, but she added that the study did have certain limitations.

On the plus side, the study examined a large number of patients, including patients from a variety of clinical environments, and it compared pregnancy results among women with and without lupus, she said. However, she added, the study relied on analyzing hospital admission and discharge data, rather than on analyzing individual patient records or on examining the patients themselves.

Lupus and Lupus Medication Affect Mood

John W. Barnhill

John W. Barnhill is the chief consultation liaison in psychiatry at the Hospital for Special Surgery in New York City and an associate professor of clinical psychiatry and public health at Weill Cornell Medical College. Barnhill explains how having lupus can affect a person's mood. For instance, because lupus is difficult to diagnose, patients might become frustrated with their doctors. Living with the symptoms of lupus can also be stressful, and for some people lupus can cause cognitive dysfunction, depression, and personality change. Various medications used to treat the disorder can also cause these and other psychological effects. Barnhill suggests that patients remain realistic about their disorder by accepting that some days will be more challenging than others. He also encourages patients to talk about their illness with others who can support them.

Lupus can have a profound effect on one's mood and outlook on life. Whether triggered by the physical symptoms of the condition itself, or as a result of side effects of medications commonly administered to

SOURCE: John W. Barnhill, summarized by Mike Elvin, "The Effects of Lupus and Lupus Medications on Mood," Hospital for Special Surgery, July 26, 2007. Reproduced by permission.

A lupus patient takes the many daily medications she needs to fight the disease. These drugs may cause psychological side effects. (**AP Images**)

lupus patients, the effects of lupus can have a marked psychological impact on those who live with it.

Lupus is a very complicated illness, and the various forms of the disease can affect people in different ways. Occasionally, this unpredictability leads to confusion, distrust, and stress.

Lupus is caused by an overactive immune system. Treatment is aimed at resetting the thermostat of the immune system so it's not overreacting without causing major side effects; in short, the goal is to try to return the immune system to being normal. Occasionally, however, there will be unpredictable effects of a medication. . . .

The Impact of Symptoms

Lupus presents in so many different ways that it is known as "the great imitator." The broad range of symptoms can confuse both patients and their primary

PERSPECTIVES ON DISEASES AND DISORDERS

physicians, and so an initial diagnosis is often very difficult to make.

Further, even when the diagnosis is made, it isn't possible to precisely anticipate the course of the illness. Delays in diagnosis and the unpredictability of symptoms tend to frustrate patients and can reduce their confidence in their medical teams.

An additional frustration relates to the fact that many of the symptoms of lupus are the sorts of aches, pains, and fatigue that are common among people who don't have lupus. People with lupus are, therefore, faced with further uncertainty: Is their symptom related to lupus, or can it be chalked up to aging or a completely unconnected ailment?

This uncertainty can lead people with lupus to worry that every symptom is a sign of SLE [systemic lupus erythematosus] and to have problems believing their medical team when they say not to be concerned. Such uncertainty can also lead to vague, chronic worry about health and can interfere with the ability to make plans for the future.

Stress and Lupus

Is lupus caused by stress? The short answer is "no." While stress may appear to set off lupus flares, there hasn't yet been evidence to indicate that stress, in itself, is enough to cause lupus or a lupus flare.

This clinical evidence is important in that some people might blame themselves for their lupus, believing that their stress might have caused the lupus. Such a rationalization is very human and understandable, but the reality is that our understanding of the cause of lupus is incomplete but that it does appear that lupus is not caused by psychological factors.

There is some biological evidence of links between stress and lupus flares. Such research focuses on B and T suppressor cells [cells that help fight infection], cytokines [proteins thought to cause fatigue], and various types of antibodies [proteins used by the immune system]. It should be noted, however, that these research findings are interesting but have not yet been shown to have clinical, practical relevance.

While stress does not seem to be a primary cause for lupus, it is clear that lupus causes people stress through its physical effects, its related uncertainty, and the resulting worries about physical problems.

Direct Complications of SLE

Lupus can directly affect thinking, mood, and personality. When it has these effects, it is called *neuropsychiatric lupus*. Symptoms of neuropsychiatric lupus include:

- *Cognitive dysfunction:* Refers to a variety of related experiences, including forgetfulness, worry, mistrust, and a general difficulty in thinking. Some people with lupus describe feeling "fuzzy-headed" or being in a "lupus fog." Often mild and reversible, cognitive dysfunction is commonly seen during lupus flares. These feelings are experienced by those without lupus as well, of course, and are perfect examples of the difficulty physicians face in diagnosing lupus.
- *Depression and anxiety:* May occur as direct effect of the lupus, as a psychological reaction to the illness, or as a reaction to medications used to treat lupus. Mood symptoms also occur commonly in people without lupus, and so it is generally difficult to be certain about what causes depression and anxiety in people with lupus.
- *A personality change:* This can refer to feelings of anger, irritability, and lability (the sensation of not feeling or acting like yourself). The unpredictability of these changes makes it hard for some people with lupus to connect with those around them. They may even wonder if their communication problems are the result of their friends and loved ones reacting poorly to their condition.

Lupus Is Linked to Depression and Anxiety Disorders

A study in the journal *Arthritis and Rheumatism* surveyed 326 white women with systemic lupus erythematosus (SLE). Of the 326 participants, 211 met the criteria for at least one of the lifetime depressive or anxiety disorders, below.

The investigators found that major depression, bipolar disorder, panic disorder, specific phobia, and obsessive-compulsive disorder were significantly more common among SLE subjects than among other white women.

In contrast, generalized anxiety disorder and mild depression were significantly less common in SLE patients.

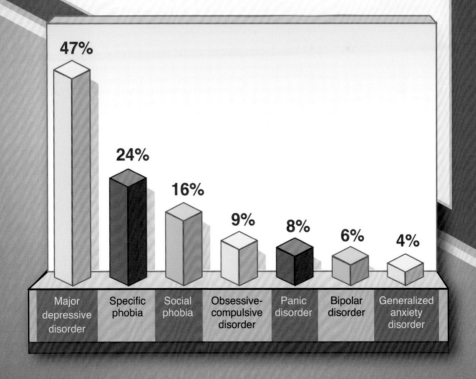

Major depressive disorder	Specific phobia	Social phobia	Obsessive-compulsive disorder	Panic disorder	Bipolar disorder	Generalized anxiety disorder
47%	24%	16%	9%	8%	6%	4%

Using Steroids to Treat SLE

Steroids are often central to the treatment of lupus, but steroids such as prednisone can cause all of the symptoms of neuropsychiatric lupus. Because neuropsychiatric symptoms are common in SLE, terms have sprung up that are widely used but are also often inaccurate.

"Steroid psychosis" is a term that some use for the emotional effects of steroids. It should be emphasized, however, that steroids don't commonly cause psychosis, but more often cause milder emotional changes, such as anxiety or depression. The term "lupus cerebritis" is used to specifically refer to the effects of lupus itself on the brain.

In trying to distinguish the cause of neuropsychiatric symptoms, it is useful to recall that lupus is *more likely* to be the cause than steroids when:

- It has been more than two weeks after an increase in prednisone
- The prednisone dose was less than 40 milligrams per day
- The emotional symptoms improve with additional steroids.

Biology of Neuropsychiatric Symptoms

Those with lupus may wonder how their condition can directly and biologically cause problems with thinking and mood.

Often, there is a direct neurological involvement in lupus related to the autoimmune system. There remains controversy about how lupus affects the brain. Antineuronal antibodies (antibodies against nerve tissue) have been demonstrated, but it is not yet clear whether these antibodies cause direct damage to the nerves. We know that patients with lupus, on no steroids, can have depression, delirium, confusion, mistrust, and even psychosis.

Anti-phospholipid antibodies are also present in some patients with lupus. Anti-phospholipid antibodies don't seem to cause inflammation, but rather are involved with increased clotting risk, and can be associated with stroke and cognitive problems.

Many of these neuropsychiatric effects are reversible, and there is a much lower risk of developing these problems if a patient with lupus only has joint and skin involvement, if the patient is ANA-negative [negative for antinuclear antibodies] or if the illness is a the result of medication, which can be withdrawn.

The Psychological Impact of SLE

People react to having lupus in different ways, and these reactions can change with time. Some of these reactions may include:

- Grief
- Depression
- Anxiety
- Regression and reduced independence (due to physical limitations, etc.)
- Isolation and social withdrawal (due to unpredictable moods, a prominent rash, etc.)
- Fears of worsening disease and disability
- Fears of cognitive problems, stroke, kidney failure, becoming a burden, etc.

It is important to note, however, that along with these "negative" reactions, those in the lupus community have rallied around each other to promote the positive effects of taking part in their shared experience. Feelings of pride, endurance, connection, appreciation, and maturity have also been commonly seen in people with lupus. . . .

Ways to Improve the Negative Effects of SLE

While it's important [for lupus patients] to try to focus on the positive, it's equally important to accept that certain days will be difficult and that merely trying to remain positive may not be enough. As one [patient] puts it, "you can live with it for years and years, and some times are better than others."

"Be honest with yourself," adds another [patient]. "Sometimes, it's too much to ask to put on a front."

"Sometimes I find myself spinning my own wheels, staying angry," another [patient] explains, "spending too much time on the Internet overdiagnosing myself, driving myself crazy. I had to tell myself not to obsess on the computer. Sit back. Get a different perspective."

One way to get a new perspective is [for patients] to reach out for help and accept that it's okay to do so. . . . A major benefit of talking with others who share [patients'] experiences is to understand which tools they use in their "toolbox." Each person has his or her own way of making their situation better, whether it's a technique such as muscle relaxation, yoga, TV watching, or reading.

Lupus Can Be Treated with Natural Remedies

Aimee Magrath

Aimee Magrath is a family naturopath, a clinician who uses natural remedies to treat various ailments. A lupus sufferer herself, Magrath specializes in treating lupus, chronic fatigue syndrome, and allergies, and she is an accredited member of the Australian Traditional Medicine Society. In this article Magrath outlines the ways in which natural remedies may benefit lupus sufferers when used in conjunction with traditional treatments. Natural herbs and minerals can help boost energy, suppress inflammation and joint pain, promote liver health and immune system regulation, and even balance hormones. Magrath also recommends physical therapy and exercise for lupus patients, and she stresses that emotional well-being is also important.

Diagnosed with SLE [systemic lupus erythematosus] at the age of 13, I understand the daily battles that lupus sufferers can go through. Extreme fatigue, joint pains and sore throats, were among

SOURCE: Aimee Magrath, "Treating Lupus with Natural Therapies," NaturalTherapyPages.com, June 30, 2008. Reproduced by permission of the author.

Use of Alternative Medicine Is on the Rise

A 2007 poll conducted by the National Institutes of Health (NIH) and the Centers for Disease Control and Prevention (CDC) showed a slight increase in the percentage of adults using complementary and alternative medicine (CAM) treatments. The government had not kept track of CAM records since 2002.

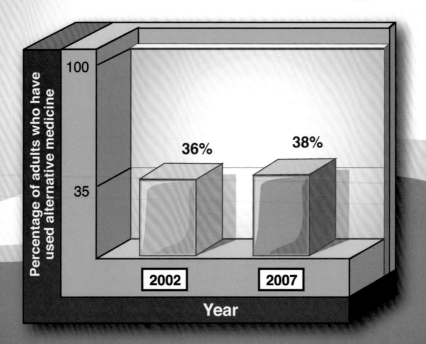

Taken from: Lara Endreszi, "New Poll Shows Use of Alternative Medicine on the Rise," Health News, December 11, 2008. www.healthnews.com/natural-health/alternative-medicine/new-poll-shows-use-alternative-medicine-rise-2256.html.

the myriad of symptoms interfering with my schooling and previously active life. In my struggle to regain good health, I discovered natural therapies and have never looked back. Now, more than 15 years on since my diagnosis, I am a qualified naturopath and nutritionist, have been medication-free for over ten years, managing my condition with a combination of natural therapies.

Using natural therapies to treat lupus can be highly successful for many patients. As every lupus patient is different, the right combination of treatments must be found for each individual. Finding that right combination can be a challenge, and can only come from [patients'] own experiences, working with a qualified practitioner who can guide [them] in the right direction as well as patience and commitment.

A balanced approach is the best way to tackle lupus, using appropriate natural therapies that work in conjunction with medical treatment. It is important [for lupus patients] to be under the care of a specialist or GP [general practioner], who can monitor [their] condition and order medical tests as required, and [they] should keep both [their] doctor and [their] natural health practitioner informed of any medications and supplements [they] are taking.

Nutrition

The basis of treatment for any chronic condition is good nutrition. A balanced diet based on wholegrains, fresh fruit and vegetables and filtered water is essential, with as little as possible of fried foods and processed foods such as biscuits and cakes.

Specific foods to avoid include alfalfa (as it can cause lupus flares), artificial sweeteners and excessive dairy products and red meat as these can encourage inflammation in the body. Plants from the "nightshade family"—potato, tomato, capsicum, eggplant and chilli—contain a substance called solanine, which can interfere with enzymes in the muscles and may cause pain and discomfort in sensitive people. Testing and consequent treatment for food intolerances can also be helpful.

Foods to include in the diet are garlic, onions, celery, cinnamon, berries, ginger, turmeric, oily fish, fresh

Dairy products are one of the specific food groups to avoid when planning proper nutrition for lupus patients. (© Photononstop/ Superstock)

pineapple and fresh papaya which contain enzymes that reduce swelling, inflammation and pain.

Energy

Magnesium can help reduce fatigue and muscle pain, as well as relieve headaches and stress. Food sources of magnesium include wholegrains, nuts, leafy green vegetables and legumes. A magnesium supplement is often more effective, aim for 200–300mg per day. Coenzyme Q10 can also be beneficial, and if blood tests show that [a patient is] iron deficient, a good iron supplement will lift [his or her] energy levels.

Inflammation and Joint Support

Omega-3 essential fatty acids primarily help reduce inflammation and pain, but as well, they can improve skin health, reduce depression and improve brain function, cardiovascular and immune health. Sources include oily fish, nuts, linseeds, avocado, or fish oil or flaxseed oil supplements. Other supplements that can help reduce inflammation and support joint health include glucosamine, chondroitin, MSM [methylsulfonylmethane], bromelain, boswellia and ginger. Topical ointments and liniments can give symptomatic relief, such as tiger balm or zen liniment.

Liver Health

In naturopathy, the liver and digestive system are often looked upon as being a contributor to many chronic illnesses, and so improving liver and digestive function are often key priorities. Simple ways to help boost liver function are drinking the juice of half a lemon in warm water first thing [in the] morning or taking 1 tspn [teaspoon] of apple cider vinegar in warm water before meals. Herbs that can be useful to improve liver function include Cynara (Globe Artichoke), Dandelion Root and St. Mary's Thistle, however it is best to seek professional advice before taking these herbs, as they can interact with medications.

Immune Regulation

Herbs are wonderful for treating lupus and tailor-made liquid tonics can be adapted to [patient] needs. Astragalus is one of my favourite herbs for this condition as it helps to balance out and regulate the immune system.

Hormone Balancing

Many female lupus patients often have hormonal imbalances, evident by irregular periods, very heavy painful periods, prolonged PMS [premenstrual syndrome] or severe menopause symptoms. As the liver is responsible for breaking down hormones, improving liver function and digestion often balances the hormones indirectly. The herb Vitex is often useful as a hormone regulator, but this is best used under the supervision of a practitioner.

Physical Therapies and Exercise

Massage, acupuncture and shiatsu are great for keeping the circulation going and reducing pain. Gentle exercise done at [one's] own pace such as yoga, walking, swimming and chi kung keep the body mobile and muscles supple, and can help relieve tension and stress without draining energy.

Emotional Support and Stress Reduction

Emotional and mental health play a large part in any chronic illness, and because of the negative impact stress can have on the immune system, it is vital that stress is minimised. Having supportive family and friends who can offer both an ear to listen, and practical help when required is essential. The Lupus Association of NSW [New South Wales, Australia's most populous state] provides great support, literature, informative seminars and other resources to its members. [Patients should] choose health care professionals that [they] feel rapport with, so [they] will feel comfortable to ask questions and voice concerns. Counselling or creative outlets such as art or writing can greatly help the expression of emotions. Supplements such as B vitamins can help with stress, as can herbs such as Oats, St. Johns Wort (not to be used with medications), Rhemannia and Licorice (not with high blood pressure). Flower essences come in a range of different types suited to support different emotional states and can be taken as drops under the tongue or mixed in with liquid herbal formulas.

Natural therapies can be very effective as a sole treatment or alongside conventional medicine in the treatment of lupus. As certain herbs can interact with medications, [patients should] consult with a qualified practitioner before taking any herbal medications.

Popular Culture Is Becoming More Aware of Lupus

PR Newswire

Hired by nongovernmental organizations, corporations, and public relations firms, PR Newswire delivers news and multimedia content. As presented in this viewpoint, Kerri Strug has helped the Lupus Foundation of America launch an awareness campaign. The efforts of two young girls dealing with lupus caught the Olympic gold medalist's attention and inspired her to encourage the girls in their effort to raise awareness of the disease.

It was their love of sports that bonded the friendship between two young female athletes ages 11 and 13. However, it was the autoimmune disease lupus that brought Aiden Gallagher and Una-Marie Antczak together to become advocates with Olympic Gold Medalist Kerri Strug for greater understanding of the disease. Together they have launched a national effort to raise awareness of lupus by distributing purple lupus wristbands as the official national symbol for lupus awareness.

SOURCE: PR Newswire, December 17, 2004. Copyright © 2004 PR Newswire Association LLC. Reproduced by permission.

Famous People with Lupus

- Ferdinand Marcos, former Philippine dictator, who died of lupus in 1989.

- Flannery O'Connor, American fiction writer, who died of lupus in 1964.

- Hugh Gaitskell, British politician.

- Baseball player Tim Raines has played for six Major League teams, including the Montreal Expos, Chicago White Sox, New York Yankees, Oakland Athletics, Baltimore Orioles, and Florida Marlins. He is considered one of the top leadoff hitters and base runners in baseball history.

- Elaine Paige, British actress and singer.

- Seal, a British musician, had discoid lupus in his childhood.

- Charles Kuralt, former anchor of *CBS Sunday Morning*.

- Actor Ray Walston, probably best known for his portrayal of Uncle Martin on the 1960s TV sitcom *My Favorite Martian* and as Judge Henry Bone on the 1990s television show *Picket Fences*. Died 2001.

- J Dilla, a hip-hop producer and beat maker.

- Kelly Drury, model and actress, most notably on *General Hospital*.

- Caroline Dorough-Cochran, sister of Howie D. of the Backstreet Boys, who founded the Dorough Lupus Foundation in her memory.

- Mercedes Yvette (also known as Mercedes Scelba-Shorte), runner-up in season two of the reality television series *America's Next Top Model*.

- Sophie Howard, a British glamour model.

- Leslie Hunt, singer/songwriter and finalist of reality television show *American Idol* Season 6 (2007).

- Lauren Schuler Donner, Hollywood film producer.

- Kelly Stone (sister of actress Sharon Stone) diagnosed with SLE.

- Pietra Thornton, former wife of Billy Bob Thornton and former Playboy model.

Raising Awareness for Lupus

While undergoing treatment for lupus, which causes inflammation and tissue damage to various parts of the body, Aiden and Una-Marie made a pact to do whatever they could to educate the public about the potentially devastating health effects of this chronic disease. The girls decided to distribute wristbands to tell people "someone you know has lupus." Approximately 1.5 million Americans, mostly women, have a form of the disease.

Their efforts immediately captured the attention of Olympic Gold Medalist Kerri Strug, who serves as a national sports celebrity for the Lupus Foundation of America (LFA). Inspired by the girls' determination and endurance, Kerri Strug met with Aiden and Una-Marie to encourage them to believe in their goal, just as she did to overcome a painful injury and help her gymnastics team capture the Olympic gold medal during the 1996 Atlanta games. On December 16, at the Hospital for Special Surgery in New York City, Aiden and Una-Marie presented Kerri with the first official lupus awareness purple wristband.

FAST FACT

May is Lupus Awareness Month.

Una-Marie and Aiden share a love of athletics. Una-Marie is an avid figure skater and Aiden plays softball, soccer and rides horses. While lupus-related fatigue and joint pain, and the side effects of the medicines they take to combat the disease, have affected their athletic endeavors for the time being, in the minds of others with lupus the girls already are gold medal champions for their efforts to increase awareness of the disease.

Aiden, of Poughkeepsie, New York, and Una-Marie, of Bayonne, New Jersey, are distributing the purple wristbands to their classmates at their respective schools to increase awareness and raise funds to support lupus research,

The TV show *House*, starring Hugh Laurie (pictured), has raised public awareness of lupus through humor. A running joke in the series has Laurie's character repeatedly misdiagnosing lupus. (Fox-TV/The Kobal Collection/The Picture Desk, Inc.)

education, and services of the Lupus Foundation of America. Aiden and Una-Marie want all people with lupus across America to join their efforts. Purple is the official color of the LFA, the nation's leading nonprofit voluntary health organization dedicated to finding the causes and cure for lupus.

Wristbands are available through the LFA's website store at http://www.lupus.org/, and through the LFA's national network of 250 chapters, branches and support groups. For more information about lupus and a list of local LFA chapters, visit the LFA website or call 1-888-38-LUPUS.

CHAPTER 3

Personal Narratives

Three Teens Talk About Living with Lupus

Patrick Hayes

Patrick Hayes is a staff writer for Lupus Now, a publication of the Lupus Foundation of America. In this viewpoint Hayes interviews three active teens with lupus about the special problems their disorder creates for them in the summer. The teens have all learned to avoid the summer sun or to take extra precautions while participating in outdoor activities to avoid lupus flare-ups. While lupus sometimes puts a crimp in their summer fun, these teens agree that they feel best when they listen to their own bodies and do not push themselves beyond their individual limits. The teens also say that their friends are inevitably understanding and sympathetic when they need to take a break from summer activities.

Photo on previous page. Thousands march in Kuala Lumpur, Malaysia, to raise public awareness of lupus. The umbrellas symbolize the need for lupus sufferers to avoid the sun's rays. (Bazuki Muhammad/Reuters/Landov)

F or many teenagers, summertime means no school, long, lazy days and fun times spent at the beach, at camps, and on family vacations. For teens with lupus, however, this fun time can be tempered by symptoms brought on by sun exposure and wanting to fill each day with activities. It can also be intimidating to tell

SOURCE: Patrick Hayes, "Shades of Summer," *Lupus Now*, Summer 2008. Reproduced by permission.

friends that you can't do certain things because of lupus. . . . We asked three teenagers how they manage having fun in the summer without taking on too much. We talked to Susan B., 14, from Independence, KY; Gloriana DeCandia, 15, from Ventura, CA; and Soha Gilani, from Abqaiq, Saudi Arabia, 14, who all have lupus.

Lupus Now: Is it difficult telling friends you can't participate in certain activities? What can you do in the summertime?

Soha: For me, it is not difficult at all. My friends are very understanding. There aren't many things I can do during the summer, but indoor swimming is a possibility. I tend to stay away from outdoor activities in the summer, so going to the beach or playing volleyball outside are activities I can't partake in; mostly I just stay indoors and maybe play basketball or go bowling.

Gloriana: It's usually not a problem—friends understand if you just explain it to them. Most are considerate and work around it. I can basically do everything; I just have to set limits for myself. If I go to the beach, I'll sit under an umbrella and make sure I have plenty of sunscreen on. I go swimming—I just have to pace myself, and take breaks sitting in the shade for a little bit.

Susan: Most of my friends don't know I have lupus because my symptoms have been so mild, but when I do tell them, they are sympathetic. I do most all of the normal summer stuff. I like to go swimming; I'll just put on a lot of sunscreen to be safe. I have occasional joint pain, so swimming is good because it doesn't bother my joints.

What kinds of activities present difficulties for you in the summertime? How do you handle it when your friends want to do these things?

Soha: I miss going to the pool or going sunbathing, and I get especially mad when our school hosts events at water parks. But I try to make everyone understand my situation and make a compromise—instead of spending a morning at the beach, how about going at sunset and making a bonfire?

Teens with Lupus Know Their Limits

How did you first figure out what you're not able to do?
Was it a specific incident when you were younger?

Gloriana: When I first learned I had lupus, I did exactly as the doctor told me about going outside. But then I started doing my own thing, and the day after being out in the sun, I wouldn't feel too well. I think, little by little, you do stupid things like that and you figure out you should go by what the doctor says.

Susan: Just before I was diagnosed, I was visiting one of my aunts and I got really sick because I was out in the sun a lot.

Is it difficult telling yourself, "OK, I need to sit this one out?"

Susan: It's not really an issue. My mom is always nagging me to put on sunscreen and I'm always like, "Mom, I don't want to," but I have to take time to put on sun-

Individuals with lupus cannot participate in outdoor activities such as beach volleyball because exposure to the sun can bring on symptoms of the disease. (Dennis MacDonald/Alamy)

screen and do other things so I can participate in summer activities. There also have been times when I didn't want to take a break, but if I have to sit something out, I just try to let [my frustration] go.

Soha: For me, it most certainly is. This year is my last year in my school and next year I will be going to boarding school, so I wanted to participate in everything. When track season came around, I didn't join. Then, I discussed the issue with my parents and doctor and they all agreed that I could run, but I had to be very careful. The doctor told me to run short distances and sprints because short distances only take up to one minute. So, that's what I did—I only ran the 100-meter, which took me about 15 seconds. That isn't too much exposure to sun. I'm also lucky that the track where we practice every day is shaded, so I was able to train with my team.

> **FAST FACT**
>
> More than ten thousand children in the United States are living with lupus.

Gloriana: I've had lupus for so long that I kind of understand now if I have to miss out on a party because I'm not feeling good, or if I won't be able to go somewhere because I can feel a flare-up coming on. It's what I've got to do to stay healthy.

A Doctor's Perspective

We spoke with Peter Chira, M.D., a pediatric rheumatologist at Lucile Salter Packard Children's Hospital at Stanford University in Palo Alto, CA, to find out what advice he has for teens.

> Teens with lupus should understand their particular symptoms of lupus—everybody's a little bit different. Often we'll say that you shouldn't be out in the sun or be stressed out, but there isn't one set guideline for saying "nobody should do x, y, z . . ." .
>
> A lot of the kids are really young when they first present with their lupus, so they don't know what their initial

manifestations were. One of the crucial things, especially for teenagers, is trying to figure out if they remember what they went through—did they go through chemotherapy? Were they hospitalized? If they can identify what their initial manifestations and symptoms were, they can identify what will trigger a flare-up.

To explain how they're feeling, teens with lupus could tell their friends, "Remember when you had the flu, how you felt with that? There are times that I feel like I have the flu every single day of my life. You look at me and I do everything, but that flu feeling is always inside of me." The flu is something that their friends can understand. If they can get that empathy, their friends can understand things a little bit better.

Most people are fairly understanding. For teens with lupus, it's about overcoming a fear and misconception that other kids don't want to understand. Kids do want to understand. They want to know what their friends are going through and, while they may not go through it themselves, I've found that they're empathetic and sympathetic if their friend has limitations caused by having lupus.

A Professional Baseball Player Battles Lupus

New York Post

The *New York Post* is self-described as the nation's oldest continuously published daily newspaper. Baseball player Tim Raines talks to the *Post* about his struggle with lupus and the influence the disease had on his baseball career with the Montreal Expos. Though the disease caused him to miss a year and a half of playing with the team, he refers to his return to the sport as a "continuation" instead of a comeback. According to Raines, he is simply doing what he was meant to do.

Even by Tim Raines' own lofty standards, what the [Montreal] Expos' outfielder has done is amazing. He has battled and beaten Lupus, a life-threatening disease that sapped his endurance and bloated his body. He's fought back to the big leagues and is batting .400 at 41, when most players are already several years into retirement. And in a city that is lukewarm about its baseball, he's become an icon, getting standing ovations with every trip to the plate.

SOURCE: *New York Post*, April 17, 2001. Copyright © 2001 NYP Holdings, Inc. All rights reserved. Reproduced by permission.

About the only person unimpressed with what Raines has done is The Rock himself.

"It's been pretty exciting. [But] I still feel like I can play at this level, and I've proven that," said Raines, whose Expos opened a three-game set at Shea [Stadium] last night [April 16, 2001]. "I don't want people to feel sorry for me [for being] 41, missing 1½ years. I don't feel like I'm doing anything special. I feel like I'm doing what I'm supposed to. Not that many guys have done it, but it doesn't mean it can't be done."

Battling Lupus

Raines spent his first dozen seasons in Montreal before winning World Series in 1996 and '98 with the Yankees. But on July 19, 1999, Oakland put him on the DL [disabled list] with a kidney inflammation. He was diagnosed with Lupus, and the 5-8, 195-pound man known as The Rock ballooned to 225 pounds. But as he was fighting for his life, he was also trying to save his career.

> **FAST FACT**
>
> Fifty percent of people with lupus develop the butterfly rash.

"Lupus took a year and a half of my career. Unfortunately things happen in your life. But I always said when I'm done, I wanted to leave on my own terms. That certainly wasn't on my own terms," said Raines, who doesn't like the word comeback, but says, "It's a continuation."

He went to spring training last year with the [Bronx] Bombers, but retired in March after injuring his foot. He tried out for the Olympic team, only to be cut at the last minute. And his playing days seemed over last August when he flew to Montreal to be inducted into the Expos' Hall of Fame. But that's when he approached them about another comeback, er, continuation.

"Getting Tim Raines has been great," said Expos manager Felipe Alou, who was the third base coach when Raines arrived in '79. "I didn't expect him to be a good player again so soon; the last Tim Raines I saw in Montreal was overweight, didn't make the Olympic team. The guy was not really a baseball player.

"But he showed up in spring training in much better shape. A lot of people thought we were trying to give him a job; but he came in, hit .400 in spring training. He made the team."

Final Goal

His last goal? Playing in the majors with his son, Tim Jr. The 21-year-old is playing Single-A ball in the Baltimore system. On March 6 [2006], they both batted leadoff for their respective teams and collected RBI [run batted in] singles.

"I hope he has a good year this year. It's pretty much up to him now, to prove that he can play at this level. Hopefully he can get up this year."

I Have Lupus, but It Does Not Have Me

Jennifer Hancock

Jennifer Hancock is a twenty-two-year-old who frequently writes opinion pieces for the *Nevada (MO) Daily Mail*. In this viewpoint Hancock writes about coming to terms with her lupus diagnosis. She says she finds support in online groups of people with lupus. Online forums allow her to share her frustrations about the disorder—and the various medical procedures she must undergo—with people who understand her. While her own family and even her supervisors at her job at Target are supportive, Hancock feels a special connection with her unique online friends who have lupus.

This column may be a little candid and frank, but there's no other way to describe or accurately talk about lupus. So brace yourself.

Hi. My name is Jennifer, and I have lupus. It's never been challenging for me to say that. I'm really good at pretending things don't bother me. In my last column I briefly mentioned how I handled things so well. I've

SOURCE: Jennifer Hancock, "I Have Lupus," *Nevada (MO) Daily Mail*, March 5, 2009. Reproduced by permission of the author.

heard, "But you look so good!" "You're so young!" And, "You don't even look sick!" No, I'm just really good at pretending. What people don't see or hear are my hysterical phone calls to mom in the middle of the night bawling that things just aren't fair. You don't see me break down in the doctor's office crying that I just want to be a "normal" kid—whatever that may be.

Don't get me wrong; the last thing I want is sympathy. I just want people to understand. I want people to know the facts about lupus. It's not pretty. It's not easy. This is my story.

Life's not fair. Don't worry; it didn't take me 22 years to figure this out. But it does hit you when you least expect it. Lupus is the same way. I can be wide-eyed and bushy tailed one second and the next I can barely keep my eyes open. When I would drive to and from Columbia and Nevada [both in Missouri], I had my roadside park where I would always stop and take a 15-minute nap.

One time during my freshman year at Mizzou [University of Missouri], my roommate Brittany walked into our dorm room and saw me crashed on the floor with my bottom dresser drawer open. I was putting laundry away and I got tired so I just lay down for a second and fell asleep. Sometimes it was really merciless trying to stay awake in class, let alone actually pay attention to what the professor was saying.

I wouldn't say I "lost" friends. I just wasn't able to explain things in a way that people could adequately understand this disease. I didn't even understand it! It's not something an 18-year-old wants to deal with unless they have to—like I do. Doctors became my best friends. They understood the uncomfortable and unnatural pain that I felt in my ribs. "Yes, that's your ribs. They are inflamed." Gee, why didn't I think of that?

The Online Community Is Like Family

The Internet is a marvelous thing. The lupus community online is a very close family. We talk to each other about the new drugs we have taken and explain the side effects that each of us has experienced.

I remember the day I found the Facebook group called "Hot Chicks with lupus." It was sensational! People my age were speaking my language! I was no longer a freak of nature.

One girl came in and welcomed me to the group. We share stories and stay in touch through Facebook. She's doing well. She received a kidney transplant last year. I remember telling my sister about it I was so thrilled for her. So when a new and scared girl came into the group, I welcomed her and gave her a heads up to what she might experience within the first months . . . new doctors and new top of the line medicines.

The author says that connecting with other lupus sufferers through Internet forums has helped her deal with problems associated with the illness. **(By Ian Miles-Flashpoint Pictures/ Alamy)**

We are part of a special, unique, and elite family. We will always be connected with the same positive antinuclear antibody test results.

Perhaps one of the most prominent people in the lupus world is a brave and incredible woman named Christine Miserandino. She is the infamous author of "The Spoon Theory." I strongly encourage everyone to go to the website www.butyoudontlooksick.com and read the Spoon Theory. It explains lupus in the most appropriate and authentic way anyone could ever put into words. The first time I read it I couldn't believe it. "Yes! Me too! Uh huh! That's me!" Needless to say I collect a lot of spoons. (When you read the story you will understand.)

> **FAST FACT**
>
> The Lupus Foundation of America holds monthly Web chats on various lupus-related topics at www.lupus.org.

Sometimes People Misunderstand Lupus

Moving out to Tucson is definitely the best thing I have done for myself. It was a chance to "start over" so to speak. I told myself that when I found my new group of friends I was going to leave out the part about having lupus. It was going to save us all a lot of questions and "I'm so sorry's!" I'd learned it wasn't a great conversation starter. It killed the mood a little.

However, when I found my friends at my job at Target, I just felt so comfortable with them that I told them everything. I don't know if it's the weather out here, but a lot more people have heard of lupus here. I hear a lot of people say that their mother, cousin, or aunt has lupus, but they don't really know much about it. Wait. You mean you've heard of lupus before? That's awesome! That's a start!

It's forgivable that my bosses and fellow team members at Target were a little leery when I would call in sick almost once a week. I had never worked a 40-hour-a-week job before. But when they read the spoon theory it was a whole new world. It was wonderful.

There will always be those who will never understand. Someone once told me that moving to Tucson would just be running from my problems. I will occasionally get the question, "So you think you can just solve things with a pill?" Oh, honey, if only lupus were that easy. I always hear "Have you ever gotten a second opinion?" Come on folks. I'm accustomed [to] the fact that I have lupus. I have nine of the 10 major symptoms. At some point I had to surrender and trust the five doctors that say I have lupus.

I hate lupus. But I have lupus. Lupus doesn't have me. Except on the days when I have bad flare ups. Then I have to cave in and listen to my incurable body. I will fight this daunting disease. I will continue to say I'm doing well when I know I just took a pill to ease my pain for the duration of the day. I don't want you to feel sorry for me. I just want you to know about my disease. I want people to know my story.

It's been one week since I had my hip replacement. In the past week I haven't bent over more than 90 degrees. I haven't slept on my right side. I have lived dependent on Stacy and mom. I have been free of arthritis pain. I'm walking wonderfully. I'm in no pain. And this time, I'm not pretending.

Using Humor to Communicate the Challenges of Lupus

Jayne

Jayne is forty years old, the mother of three, and has lupus. In addition to writing a blog on lupus on her Web site, The View from My Shoes, Jayne writes on autism, Down syndrome, special education, and other topics. Her various blogs have earned her a "Top Health Blogger" classification from WellSphere, an online health information site. In this article Jayne writes seriously, but humorously, about her struggles with butterfly rashes, joint pain, and the "brain fog" caused by her lupus. She laments turning forty and not being the healthy, active woman she expected to be, but she remains committed to finding new ways of beating the symptoms of lupus, such as yoga and relaxing getaways with her sisters. Eventually, she says, she will also muster the energy to clean her house.

Pardon my absence lately, I've been feeling pretty crappy in a Lupus kind of way. I'm really starting to hate this new addition to my life. At first I thought, "No biggie, I can handle it, I'm Super-Jayne!,"

SOURCE: Jayne Hickey, "Something's Gotta Give and Lord Don't Let It Be My Bowels," The View from My Shoes, personal blog, November 3, 2008. Reproduced by permission of the author.

now I'm realizing this thing is far bigger than me and I'm no Super-Jayne!

This butterfly rash so commonly associated with Lupus has spread its wings all over my face. It'd be one thing if it was giving me that sun-kissed look but no, in typical Jayne fashion, it's giving me the "oh my god what happened to your face?!" look.

My shoulders and neck burn like nobody's business, not sure what the heck is going on there. It radiates down my arms throughout the day, like right now as I type this.

My ankles, hips, wrists, and thumb joints feel like someone took them and beat them with a meat cleaver and ran. Nice description, I know. I struggle with words lately, this leads me to my next problem.

Brain fog. I am so forgetful, constantly going into a room and wondering what the heck it was I was going to do in there in the first place. Usually if I wait it out a few seconds, it'll come to me. Sometimes I just start doing *something* and then I recall the *original* thing I was going to do in there! I'm thinking about taking Ernie's advice and tying string around all my fingers but have a feeling I may forget what that was for in the first place. Another memory problem occurs mid conversation with someone, I just can't seem to recall the word I am searching for in my *vast* internal word resource. Worse yet, sometimes I substitute a word that isn't even close to the word I meant to say. This makes for great conversation. Just this very morning my daughter was telling me that she will get to ride in the elevator at school today because her friend has a sprained ankle and has chosen my daughter as one of two friends she could take along. She told me there are two kids in her homeroom that are riding the elevator now. I tried to ask a simple question and this is what came out, "Are they both on crackers?"

FAST FACT

Eighty percent of young women in the United States have little or no knowledge of lupus.

"I mean *crutches*!"??? My daughter got quite the chuckle out of that one. I'm sure in her head she's thinking, "um no Mom, but you've gone *crackers*!" Sweet girl kept her thoughts to herself!

Something's Got to Give

So as you can see, I'm clearly struggling with old age symptoms and will turn 40 in eleven days. I used to joke about feeling really old when I turned 40 *but it was a joke dammit*! It wasn't supposed to really happen. I was going to hit my stride, be physically fit, look great, and leave those girls from High School that everyone loved, the tan, perfect body, evenly proportioned, great hair, great smile girls, behind with their leathery skin and melanoma's and strut my stuff at my 25th High School Reunion! If I decided that was what I felt like doing. Now, I'll be lucky if I can even walk!

Some lupus sufferers are plagued with memory problems, including such things as remembering the correct words to use in conversation. (McPhoto/PST/INSADCO Photography/Alamy)

PERSPECTIVES ON DISEASES AND DISORDERS

117

Something's gotta give. I'm going to start with a little Yoga as prescribed by my wise and older sister. Maybe I can just center this thing right on out of me! Then I'm going to continue to take Mommy get-aways with my sisters for good mental health, they both *insist* on this one. I tend to agree. Gonna get that diet of mine in check as soon as I get all this darn Halloween Candy out of my pantry! I think I've eaten more than my fair share of the peanut laden items my allergic daughter can't have. Gee you think that has anything to do with my crappy skin? Um . . . but some of it was dark chocolate . . . antioxidants???

Okay, enough of my complaining. One more thing though, grant me this one. My house looks like a bomb went off in here and I really need to dig deep into my energy reserve and get it together. For me, clean home = happy home = happy Jayne! I need a maid!

GLOSSARY

antibodies	Proteins made by the body's white blood cells to defend the body against foreign enemies.
anti-inflammatory drug	A drug used to control inflammation.
antimalarials	Drugs such as Plaquenil, originally developed to treat malaria, that have beneficial effects in the treatment of lupus.
antinuclear antibodies (ANA)	Autoantibodies that attack substances found in the center, or nucleus, of all cells.
arthritis	Inflammation of a joint or joints.
autoantibody	An antibody that attacks the body's own cells or tissues.
autoimmune disorder	A condition, such as lupus, in which the immune system mistakes healthy tissues for foreign invaders and makes antibodies against them.
butterfly rash (or malar rash)	A red rash over the cheeks and the bridge of the nose.
connective tissue	The tissues that hold the body together.
corticosteroid	A natural anti-inflammatory hormone made by the adrenal glands.
cortisone	A synthetic (human-made) corticosteroid, such as prednisone, commonly used to treat lupus.
cutaneous lesions	Rashes, scarring, or sores on the skin.
discoid lupus	A type of skin disease sometimes seen in systemic lupus; it can also exist independently of systemic lupus.

flare	The symptoms of lupus reappearing or increasing.
immune system	The network of cells and tissues that work together to protect the body against foreign invaders, such as bacteria and viruses.
immunosuppressant	A drug that treats lupus by suppressing the immune system.
inflammation	The swelling, redness, heat, and pain that can occur in the joints and tissues of lupus patients.
nonsteroidal anti-inflammatory drugs (NSAID)	A group of steroid-free drugs, such as aspirin, ibuprofen, and naproxen, used to reduce inflammation.
photosensitivity	Sensitivity of the skin to ultraviolet light from the sun or other sources.
psychosis	Extremely disordered thinking accompanied by a poor sense of reality.
selective serotonin reuptake inhibitors (SSRIs)	A group of antidepressants that work by preventing the reuptake of the neurotransmitter serotonin, thus maintaining higher levels of serotonin in the brain.
systemic	Affecting the whole body.
tricyclics	The oldest group of antidepressants.

CHRONOLOGY

1833   French dermatologist Pierre Louis Alphee Cazenave coins the term *lupus erythematosus,* or LE.

1856   Austrian dermatologist Ferdinand von Hebra publishes the first illustrations of lupus erythematosus in his *Atlas of Skin Disorders.*

1866   Ferdinand von Hebra uses the metaphor of a butterfly to describe the malar rash.

1872   Moriz Kaposi (son of von Hebra) describes the systemic nature of lupus.

1885–1904   William Osler describes the heart, lung, joint, brain, kidney, and stomach symptoms associated with systemic lupus.

1902   Jonathan Hutchinson describes the photosensitive nature of the malar rash.

1908   Alfred Kraus and Carl Bohac describe pulmonary (lung) involvement in lupus.

1922   False positive test for syphilis is recognized as a common finding in systemic lupus erythematosus, or SLE.

1948   Mayo Clinic pathologist Malcolm M. Hargraves and his colleagues discover the LE cell, a white blood cell that engulfs the nucleus of another cell. This finding suggests

SLE is an autoimmune disorder. Phillip Hench discovers cortisone, one of the best drug therapies for lupus.

1950s Antinuclear antibody tests are developed. Corticosteroids are used in treatment for lupus for the first time.

1951 Antimalarials are first used in lupus treatment.

1952 Immunosuppressants are first used in lupus treatment.

1954 The Cleveland Clinic discovers drug-induced lupus.

1955 Prednisone, a derivative of cortisone, is created and approved for lupus treatment.

1955 Plaquenil (an antimalarial drug) is approved to treat lupus.

1959 Hybrid mouse discovered with lupuslike kidney disease aids lupus research.

1960s Lupus diagnostic techniques and treatments improve; public awareness of lupus begins to develop. Physician Edmund L. Dubois of Johns Hopkins University edits the first lupus textbook, *Dubois' Lupus Erythematosus*, in its seventh edition in 2009.

1970s The Lupus Foundation of America is formed.

1971 A committee of North American rheumatologists meet to establish the criteria for diagnosing SLE.

1977 President Jimmy Carter declares September 18–24 as the first National Lupus Awareness Week.

1982 The diagnostic criteria for lupus are revised to include a broader range of symptoms. National Lupus Awareness Week is moved to October.

1986 President Ronald Reagan designates October as National Lupus Awareness Month.

2004 On May 10 the first World Lupus Day is observed.

2007 The Lupus Foundation of America awards more than $1.1 million in new research grants.

2008 The Lupus Foundation of America designates May as Lupus Awareness Month.

2009 On July 20 the research group Human Genome Sciences announces that the drug Benlysta shows promise for treating lupus in clinical trials.

ORGANIZATIONS TO CONTACT

The editors have compiled the following list of organizations concerned with the issues debated in this book. The descriptions are derived from materials provided by the organizations. All have publications or information available for interested readers. The list was compiled on the date of publication of the present volume; the information provided here may change. Be aware that many organizations take several weeks or longer to respond to inquiries, so allow as much time as possible.

Alliance for Lupus Research (ALR)
28 W. Forty-fourth St.
Ste. 501
New York, NY 10036
(212) 218-2840 or
(800) 867-1743
http://lupusresearch
.org

ALR is a national voluntary health organization committed to finding better treatments for lupus and to ultimately preventing and curing the disease. The alliance supports promising research projects of scientists at prestigious universities, medical schools, and hospitals throughout the world.

American Autoimmune-Related Diseases Association, Inc. (AARDA)
22100 Gratiot Ave.
East Detroit, MI
48021
(586) 776-3900 or
(800) 598-4668
fax: (586) 776-3903
www.aarda.org

AARDA is a nonprofit voluntary health agency dedicated to bringing a national focus to the more than one hundred autoimmune diseases through education, awareness, research, and patient services.

Arthritis Foundation
PO Box 7669
Atlanta, GA 30357-
0669
(404) 872-7100 or
(800) 283-7800
www.arthritis.org

The Arthritis Foundation supports arthritis research and provides educational and other services to individuals with arthritis. The foundation provides up-to-date information on arthritis research and treatment, nutrition, alternative therapies, and self-management strategies. Information about lupus and other autoimmune and rheumatic conditions is also available on its Web site.

Lupus Canada
590 Alden Rd., Ste. 211
Markham, ON
L3R 8N2
(905) 513-0004 or
(800) 661-1468
fax: (905) 513-9516
www.lupuscanada.org

Formed in 1987, Lupus Canada is a nonprofit agency with the objectives of encouraging cooperation among the lupus organizations in Canada and promoting public awareness and general education about lupus.

Lupus Foundation of America (LFA)
2000 L St. NW
Ste. 710
Washington, DC
20036
(202) 349-1155 or
(800) 558-0121
fax: (202) 349-1156
www.lupus.org

The LFA is a national nonprofit health organization dedicated to finding the causes of and cure for lupus. The foundation helps lupus patients and their families and works to increase public awareness of the disease. The three hundred chapters of the LFA sponsor support groups and conduct programs of research, education, and advocacy.

Lupus Research Institute (LRI)
330 Seventh Ave.
Ste. 1701
New York, NY 10001
(212) 812-9881
fax: (212) 545-1843
www.lupusresearch
institute.org

The LRI is the nation's only nonprofit organization solely dedicated to novel research in lupus. The institute funds innovative research for finding more effective treatments and a cure for lupus.

National Institute of Arthritis and Musculoskeletal and Skin Diseases (NIAMS)
1 AMS Circle
Bethesda, MD 20892-3675
(301) 495-4484 or
(877) 226-4267
TTY: (301) 565-2966
fax: (301) 718-6366
www.niams.nih.gov

NIAMS, a part of the National Institutes of Health, leads the federal government research effort in arthritis and other diseases that affect the muscles, bones, joints, and skin. The NIAMS Office of Communications and Public Liaison provides health and research information for the public through the NIAMS Information Clearinghouse.

SLE Lupus Foundation
330 Seventh Ave.
Ste. 1701
New York, NY 10001
(212) 685-4118 or
(800) 745-8787
fax: (212) 545-1843
www.lupusny.org

The SLE Lupus Foundation is a voluntary organization that supports medical research to find the cause and cure of lupus and to improve its diagnosis and treatment. The foundation provides services to help people with lupus and conducts education programs to raise awareness of lupus.

FOR FURTHER READING

Books

Sheldon Paul Blau and Dodi Schultz, *Living with Lupus: The Complete Guide*. Cambridge, MA: Da Capo, 2004.

Norma J. Bogetto, *Lupus: My View After 35 Years*. Scotts Valley, CA: CreateSpace, 2009.

Iris Quintero Del Rio, *Lupus: A Patient's Guide to Diagnosis, Treatment, and Lifestyle*. Munster, IN: Hilton, 2007.

Jennifer De Sousa, *Metal Butterfly: Lupus, the Enemy That Lurked Within Me*. Bloomington, IN: iUniverse, 2007.

Waverly Evans, *Healing Lupus: Steps in a Personal Journey*. Charleston, SC: Book Surge, 2008.

David Isenberg and Susan Manzi, *Lupus*. New York: Oxford University Press, 2007.

Julie Miller, *My Life with Lupus*. Bloomington, IN: Author-House, 2008.

Phillipa Pigache, *Positive Options for Living with Lupus: Self-Help and Treatment*. Berkeley, CA: Publishers' Group West, 2006.

Daniel J. Wallace, *The Lupus Book: A Guide for Patients and Their Families*, New York: Oxford University Press, USA, 2008.

Periodicals

Business Wire, "Lupus Foundation of America (LFA) Applauds Launch of New Lupus Awareness Campaign," March 31, 2009.

Kari Haskell, "Crisis, Strain and Hope: A Family's Balancing Act," *New York Times*, January 11, 2009.

Meg Haskell, "One Dad's Dilemma," *Bangor (ME) Daily News*, June 20, 2009.

Shirley Henderson, "Living with Lupus: Although There Is No Cure, Many People Are Making Lifestyle Adjustments to Fight the Disease and Improve Their Sense of Well-Being," *Ebony*, July 2007.

Ernest Hooper, "One Girl's Refusal to Stop Life for Lupus," *St. Petersburg (FL) Times*, May 3, 2007,

Arthur Jones, "Facing Lupus with Spiritual Life Supports," *National Catholic Reporter*, November 19, 2004.

Gregory Katz, "Real 'Lucy in the Sky with Diamonds' Has Lupus," *Raleigh (NC) News & Observer*, June 15, 2009.

Kristyn Kusek Lewis, "Tired? Achy? Thirsty? The Symptoms That Trip Up Even Top Docs," *Shape*, December 2007.

Thomas H. Maugh II, "Lupus Drug Passes Key Test, Researchers Say," *Los Angeles Times*, July 21, 2009.

Newport News (VA) Daily Press, "Living with Lupus," March 31, 2009.

Jane Oppermann, "Lupus Doesn't Keep Florist Sidelined," *Arlington Heights (IL) Daily Herald*, March 20, 2006.

Andrea Peirce, "The Many Faces of Lupus," *New York Times*, March 21, 2008.

Kimberly Lord Stewart, "The Wolf at the Door: Kimberly Lord Stewart Describes Her Battle with Lupus as She Explores the Fine Line Between Western Medicine and Alternative Therapies," *Better Nutrition*, July 2005.

INDEX